Miss Jane

Speeches and Stories

Jane Gray Krutz

ISBN: 978-0-9838105-0-6
First Printing 2011
Printed in the United States of America

Cover photo courtesy Jess Setzler, AETN
AETN photos courtesy of AETN
Book design by Lorinda Gray/Ragamuffin Creative
www.ragamuffincreative.com

To order more copies, contact Jane at:
Jane Krutz
5325 Lee Avenue
Little Rock, AR 72205
501.663.5437 or 501.944.2400

Dedication

I'm grateful to all my friends and family who encouraged
me to write this book for years and years and years.

Especially my grandson Jake, my cousin Lorinda,
and my friend Jay.

Also Alice, my hairdresser and confidant of 30 years,
who knows more about me than anyone except God.

And, to my many cousins who helped make my life sing.

But I'm especially grateful to my parents
who pointed me toward God.

Foreword

IF THERE IS A BETTER STORY TELLER in Arkansas than Jane Gray Krutz, I don't know who it is. But each of her stories has a different meaning—and a distinct message about life and how we can better live it.

Jane Krutz's wonderful little book is about giving meaning to our lives. It is, as one of her friends described, "making life sing."

From the time she so beautifully recounts her early childhood, Jane's commitment to others is the dominant theme of "Miss Jane"—this special life so well lived.

Yes, a strong Christian heritage and a family deeply embedded in the Nazarene Church and its faith, Jane makes no judgments about other denominations or different religious beliefs. In fact, she is about as ecumenical as one can be. Her life has evolved around her beloved church, family, and community—and her passion for each is intense.

At seventeen, and still a high school student, she met a young soldier then stationed at Camp Robinson. She says that Ted Krutz was the "prettiest" man she had ever seen. Smitten, she had a few dates with her dashing young beau, and when he told her he was being "shipped out" to distant battlefields, Ted and Jane plead with the Little Rock school authorities to allow her to marry while still a high school student. There was a rule against high school marriages. The case was evidently so compelling that Jane's case was granted an exception because her fiancé was in the military. In 1943, Jane Gray became the young bride of Corporal Ted Krutz. Sixty-four years and three children later, Ted died. Jane had lost her best friend.

Today, at 85 and going stronger than ever, her love for public service has never diminished. Her church, business, public speaking, the Salvation Army and Prison Ministries have all occupied a space on her busy calendar. "Anything I do, I have to do more than anyone." That she has done. She has no regrets.

In 2007, the Arkansas Educational Television Network (AETN) honored her lifetime commitment and tireless efforts on behalf of public broadcasting by naming the studio at AETN in Conway as the Jane Krutz Studio. After all, in 1995, it was Jane Krutz who testified in Washington on behalf of public broadcasting, urging Congress not to eliminate federal funding for public television and radio. With her down-home humor and brilliant style, the normally staid, conservative House and Appropriations Committee gave Jane Krutz a long standing ovation.

"Please consider this," she had argued, "that of the three public educational institutions in America, public schools, public libraries, and public television, more people can be touched by public television at any given moment than by the other two put together."

For decades, Jane Krutz has been the public face of Arkansas Educational Television (PBS)...fundraising, speaking of its importance and responding with gusto to its critics.

One of Jane's chapters has been titled Busy Busy Busy. That, she has decidedly been for almost 90 years. On many occasions, I've been honored to say in her presence: "Jane Krutz, you have made Arkansas and our world a better place." What a great journey it continues to be.

—U.S. SENATOR DAVID PRYOR, RETIRED

What Others Say About Jane...

▓ *Jane Krutz is not only one of the greatest motivational and inspirational speakers in America, but her very life preaches a gospel sermon without saying a word. She lights up the room.*

—SENATOR STANLEY RUSS, RETIRED

▓ *Since I came to AETN in 1993, Jane Krutz has been a strong and continuing influence for me both professionally and personally. We have taken many long drives together representing AETN and I have learned something new and received wonderful wisdom every single time. Plus, nobody tells a better story! Jane is the best of AETN and the best of Arkansas.*

—ALLEN WEATHERLY, AETN DIRECTOR

▓ *Jane is an inspiration to people because of her "can do" attitude. Her involvement in many organizations, such as AETN, is a testimony of her desire to reach beyond herself to make her community, and her world a better place. My life would have been less complete if I had not had the privilege of knowing her and been the recipient of her love and support.*

—DR. DAN CASEY
PASTOR OF LITTLE ROCK FIRST CHURCH OF THE NAZARENE

I admire my mother for her positive outlook on life. She can always find something good in anybody. She loves God and is never, ever ashamed to testify about Him. She loves her family and she's so much fun.
—JANIE LAY, DAUGHTER

Jane and I have been friends for over thirty years. She is a blessing to AETN and her efforts have helped sustain the position AETN holds in public television today.
—BILL VALENTINE

Personality overload would be an understatement. The good Lord, when helping to make Jane, forgot to turn off the character switch when he was building her personality and that overload helped to create the gentle and caring lady that she is and Arkansas and AETN are better because of her. She speaks to viewers in a way that we can't get to our checkbooks fast enough and send those bucks to AETN to help keep public television beaming to all of Arkansas.
—NORTH LITTLE ROCK MAYOR PATRICK HENRY HAYS

Throughout her life she has set a powerful example of leadership and motivation to which we can all aspire. Her energy and generosity have made our state a better place for all of us.
—ARKANSAS GOVERNOR MIKE BEEBE

▦ *Her heart is as big as her mouth.* —CARTOONIST GEORGE FISHER

▦ *We had some great times working together to support public television. Jane is, indeed, the best volunteer ever. She has done so much for AETN and for all of public television.*
—SUSAN HOWARTH
PRESIDENT AND CEO, WEDU, TAMPA, FLORIDA

▦ *Her faithful service, her loyal commitment, and her enthusiasm for everything she does is a delight to behold. I'm grateful for her friendship. Even more grateful for the contribution she's made to AETN and the entire state of Arkansas.*
—ARKANSAS GOVERNOR MIKE HUCKABEE

▦ *Jane's support for PBS and AETN has been unprecedented. She is a great inspiration to all of us.*
—P. ALLEN SMITH
TV HOST AND GARDEN/LIFESTYLE DESIGNER

▦ *She is one of AETN's greatest advocates.*
—WAYLON HOLYFIELD, SINGER

She has been wonderful as an honest Christian woman, savvy as a businessperson, the glue of a marvelous family, and her work in charity has been amazing for many many decades.

—AUDREY BURTRUM-STANLEY
AETN VOLUNTEER

A Birthday Letter from President Bill Clinton. *I'm glad to join the Arkansas Educational television Network in wishing you a happy 85th birthday. As a volunteer for more than 40 Arkansas organizations, you have proudly upheld our nation's tradition of volunteerism. Your efforts have made a real difference in issues from community development to health care. And especially in the world of public television. Your contributions to the success of AETN and PBS have inspired audiences in homes across the state. Your work has even informed discussions locally and nationally about the long-term future of educational programming. I am pleased to hear that you are celebrating this milestone surrounded by friends, family, and colleagues who have benefited personally from your words of encouragement. If your last 45 years of advocacy tell us anything, it is the award that matters the most is the knowledge that your leadership has enriched countless lives. You have left an indelible mark on AETN and I know I speak for all Arkansans in thanking you for both your service and example. Congratulations on this happy birthday.*

—PRESIDENT BILL CLINTON

*Joy is the most infallible proof
of the presence of God in your life.*

*The first rule of good manners is
putting up with bad ones pleasantly.*

JANE'S FAVORITE SCRIPTURES:
I Thessalonians 4:13-18
Psalm 16:5-11
Romans 8:11

Contents

Introduction

AT SIX YEARS OF AGE, I started taking piano lessons from Mary Madeares, who became famous as the author of *Big Doc's Girl*. I soon knew I did not like piano lessons. It did not come easy for me and I was petrified at recital time. However, Miss Madeares also had her pupils perform in a play. She gave me the leading role as a boy (she had no boy piano pupils at the time). I remember putting my hair up under my daddy's cap and wearing my cousin's trousers and jacket. It was my first taste of show biz and I was hooked when I got a standing ovation and raves about my performance. From that day, I started giving readings and telling stories. I got my story telling talent from my father who kept people in stitches with his tales of the family's first train trip to Georgia and other humorous family stories. I've been accused of being blessed with the art of exaggeration. However, I don't exaggerate. I simply explain details, especially those leading up to the story I'm telling.

Since I have such a strong loud voice, I also got most of the lead parts in the children's church programs. We had no sound system in those days and I was the only kid who could be heard in the top balcony. By the time I was nine, I was performing on our local church radio program every Saturday morning on the Children's Hour. I emceed, read poetry and Bible stories. By age thirteen, I started taking private speech lessons from Mrs. L.A. (Jean) Allen and that is when I blossomed into a public speaker. I remained under her teaching until I was grown and married. All three of my children took lessons from her and give her credit for their ability to teach and speak in public. She had no children and I took care of her until her death in her 80s. She willed me her entire speech studio—furniture, speeches, and so forth. She thought I would carry on her work, but by that time I was in my profession of building management and did not have time to teach.

With Mrs. Allen's death, the profession of private speech teacher died in Little Rock also. To this day, no one has ever taken her place.

From that first play at the age of six, the acting bug got me. I had intended to go to drama school to become a legitimate stage actress. That is, until I met Ted Krutz, had a family, and settled down as a wife and mother. But I've been able to fulfill that ambition with my speaking. It has taken me across the nation—from coast to coast into every church denomination and many civic organizations. From children's groups to seniors and even before Congress. Hopefully, I have encouraged others with my words.

P.S.—Under six different teachers, I never learned how to play the piano!

JANE KRUTZ
Speaker - Encourager

5325 Lee Avenue
Little Rock, AR 72205   501-663-5437

Jane Gray Krutz

14

CHAPTER 1

Family

This speech was first delivered at a Mother/Daughter Banquet for my daughter Vikki's church in Poplar Bluff, Missouri. It is a tribute to my mother, Fannie Gray, and has become one of my most requested speeches. I have often given it as the sermon in church on Sunday. Parents have told me changes were made in their parenting after hearing it.

TO GOD BE THE GLORY!

PROVERBS 22:6

The Apple of His Eye

Helping children understand the principles of God

THERE IS NOT A PERSON TODAY who does not have the privilege of being an influence on a child who comes across your path. Perhaps you're a grandparent—no one has the influence on children that grandparents have. Or perhaps you're an aunt or uncle. The nieces and nephews in your life can be one of your greatest joys. And you can be one of their greatest assets.

My aunts and uncles loved me so much when I was growing up that I just knew if anything happened to my mama or daddy they would fight over who got to raise me. That's how much they loved me. And it meant a lot to my self-worth and self-esteem the way my aunts and uncles loved me—so don't you take for granted the nieces and nephews in your life. Perhaps you're a teacher or just a neighbor that has a child under your influence…be sure to reach out to them with love.

Butterfly Sandwiches

WHEN MY SON, TEDDY, was six years old there was a family who lived a couple of doors down from us. They had a boy, Donny, who was Teddy's age, and three younger girls—still in diapers. The mother took in ironing to help with finances. Donny came down every day after school to play with Teddy. I always fixed them a snack—usually butterfly sandwiches. To make a butterfly sandwich, cut the sandwiches into triangles and put the corners together for the wings. Decorate the top with raisins or nuts. Put a piece of carrot down the middle for the body. Kids will eat healthy sandwiches if they look like a butterfly. I gave them a glass of milk or juice. Donny always ate like he was hungry—sometimes taking seconds. I also talked to him a lot. I would tell him what a handsome and smart boy he was. I told him that he could do anything in life if he just studied, worked hard, and served the Lord. I told him this over and over.

A year later they moved away. I didn't hear from them until years later when I received an invitation to his parent's 25th wedding anniversary party. It was at a small church about twenty miles out in the country. I went because I wanted to see Donny. When I got there and saw the parents and the three girls, I asked about Donny. His mother said he would be there soon. They had to fly in. A few minutes later, in walked this fine-looking family. A tall handsome man, a beautiful wife, and three handsome children. The mother said, "There is Donny now."

I said, "Why he looks like a Philadelphia lawyer."

"He is a lawyer and a very successful one."

When Donny saw me, he hugged me and kissed me and then turned to his family saying, "Kids, this is the Butterfly Sandwich lady."

"You really exist? He has talked about you all of our lives!" We had a big laugh about it.

Later, his wife called me to the side and said, "Mrs. Krutz, you will never know what you have meant to Donny. He had to work two jobs to put himself through college and law school. He would get so weary and tired he would nearly give up and quit. Then, he would remember what you told him—that he could do anything if he studied and worked hard and served the Lord. Then, he would try again until he finally got his degree. He gives you credit for his success. You will never know how often you fed him when he was hungry and what your words meant to him. He also told me that when we married I had to make butterfly sandwiches for the other kids in the neighborhood. It would be a requirement for his wife. And, I've been making them through the years."

Folks, look around you for a child to reach out to with love.

Victor and Fannie

MY MOTHER WAS 12 YEARS OLD when she first laid eyes on my father standing on a street corner in Vilonia, Arkansas. She turned to her sister and said, "That is the boy that I'm going to marry." When she was seventeen and he was eighteen, they married.

Fannie was beautiful. She was a soft, delicate lady. I see her in shades of pink. She was a very talented artist who painted china and lingerie and landscapes and portraits in oil. She played the piano and she sang high soprano.

Victor was big and strong and handsome and a loud-mouthed gregarious man. And he sang deep bass. Well, they gave their talent to the Lord. Playing the piano and singing in church. That was the way they gave their volunteer services.

Mother Fannie Diffee Gray

Father Victor Gray

Jane at the age of one

Jane at six months and mother

They were very disappointed soon after they married when the doctor told Mother that she would probably never be able to have a child. They accepted it and went on with their life.

Seven years later, the doctor said, "Miracle of miracles, Mrs. Gray! You and Victor are going to have a baby."

Mother was so thrilled that she parked her Model-T Ford on Front Street, the main street of Conway Arkansas, stopped every man, woman, and child and said, "Victor and I are going to have a baby!"

You've got to remember, this was 1925 and women didn't talk about being "in the family way" but my Mother was so thrilled that it did not matter and she told everyone.

I was the only child they ever had but I was their boy and girl rolled into one. Mother dressed me in laces and satins. She hand-painted roses around the bottom of all my little dresses and she put bonnets on me and hand-painted flowers on them. I was her princess.

I was Papa's tomboy. He put me in bibbed overalls with a billed cap and put me in the front seat of his Model-T Ford and carried me off to work with him. I was everything they ever wanted rolled into one and I was just about perfect as far as they were concerned.

I was perfect in every way except my hair. I had snow-white hair. I was a tow-head kid. It was as straight as the top of a table and it stood up all over my head. I can remember growing up, Mama licking her fingers trying to lay my hair down. In fact, she kept caps on me until I started school so that people would not see my hair.

This was OK most of the time until Aunt Effie and Cousin Doris came to visit. Cousin Doris was three months older than I was and she was a brunette Shirley Temple. She had black ringlets all over her head and every time they came, Aunt Effie would say, "Isn't it too bad about Jane's hair. Isn't it pitiful that she couldn't have pretty hair like Doris?"

Mother took this as long as she could take it and one day Aunt Effie called and said they were coming and Mama decided to curl my hair.

In those days, they didn't have electric curling irons. All they had were the curling irons that you stuck in the fire. You got it red-hot and that's what you curled hair with.

Mother sat me up on the kitchen cabinet. I was four years old and I can see it today. She got that iron hot in that gas jet and she was just fixing to put it in my hair when Daddy walked in the room. He grabbed me off that kitchen counter and said, "Fannie, have you lost your mind? Don't you know that you'll burn that little scalp with that red-hot iron?"

She said, "Victor, I can't help it. Effie's coming and she's going to make fun of Jane's hair. I can't stand it and I'm going to curl it."

He said, "You are not. I like her hair straight. In fact, I ordered it that way.

"You did?"

"Yes, I ordered her hair straight and her voice loud because I knew she was going to look exactly like you and I wanted something about her to be like me. That's the way that I ordered her. I like her just the way she is."

Mama began crying and loving me and said, "Oh, honey, I love you just the way you are. It doesn't matter how you look. It doesn't matter about your hair. Mother thinks you are wonderful also!"

And that's the way they raised me. That is the way that they loved me. And I knew that it did not matter to them that I was not perfect, or my hair was straight or my teeth were far apart in front and never would grow together. It didn't matter that I was so clumsy that I couldn't even ride a bicycle or that under five teachers I would never learn to play the piano. It didn't even matter that I was the loudest-mouthed kid on the block. I *knew* that I *knew* that I *knew* that if they had lined me up with all the kids in the world in a straight line and said "pick one" that they would have chosen me. I just knew that. Why? Because they *loved* me. They had *made* me and I was the *apple of their eye.*

I knew that I could have broken their heart. I could have done something that would have killed them but I knew without a shadow of a doubt that they would love me anyway. Their love for me was unconditional. It did not depend upon my performance.

How do you expect a child to understand the unconditional love of God—a God he has never seen or touched if his own parents and own grandparents do not love him that way? But because mine did love me and love me unconditionally, I understand a God who loves me regardless of who I am or what I do. If I'm ugly or pretty. If I'm dumb or smart. If I'm rich or poor. If I'm a failure or a success, He loves me anyway. Why?

Because He *created* me. He *loves* me. He *chose* me and I am the *apple of His eye.*

DON'T YOU EVER BE AFRAID to tell your child how wonderful they are. Affirm your love for that child. Brag on them every time you get a chance. If you want to really mess a kid up...and a child psychiatrist will tell you this...just point out every thing they do wrong all the time.

If they make two As on their report card, tell them they should have made four if they hadn't been so dumb. If they make a three-bagger at a ballgame, you tell them they could have made a home run if they hadn't been so lazy or so clumsy. Just point out everything they do wrong if you want to mess them up.

Some people say, "I don't ever brag on my child because I don't want them to be conceited." You do realize that God set the greatest example in the world for bragging on a child when Jesus was baptized. When He came up out of the water God said for the entire world to hear, "This is my beloved Son in whom I am well pleased." And don't you know during the next three years of His life, when He was being spat upon and beaten and screamed at and treated the way He was treated—don't you know that He remembered that day when His Father bragged on Him and He would probably say, "They may not like me but my Father thinks I'm wonderful."

And that's the way you should raise your child because they are going to run into some ugly things and ugly people out there in the world and you need to leave them with such a knowledge that they are loved above anything anyone else could say.

Alvin Pearce said, "Parents need to fill a child's bucket of self-esteem so high that the rest of the world can't poke enough holes in it to drain it dry." So that's why you should affirm your child and express the love you have for him.

Though my parents loved me without question, they demanded obedience. They laid down rules and they saw to it that I kept them. They dared to discipline a long time before James Dobson ever wrote a book on the subject.

They didn't beat me. They didn't abuse me—but I danced several little jigs at the end of a keen switch when I was real little. But you see, that's the secret. You do it when they are real young, and when they are real young—they learn the consequences of misbehaving. If you discipline them in diapers, you won't have a "problem teenager" on your hands. But if you wait until they are a teen to discipline them, they will be whipping you before it's over. You have to start when they are young.

The objective of discipline, the switches, and the groundings is to teach *respect* for *authority* and this is a very strong principle of God all through the Bible. If you don't teach that kind of respect while they are in the home, they will grow up and never have respect for their teachers, for the law, for their boss, for their spouse, and they will certainly not learn to respect God if you don't teach it to them.

Mamas and Papas, it is *trouble* to discipline. It's hard work. It's easier to just let them go and do whatever they want to do because it takes an effort to know who their friends are and who they are running around with. You need to know what kind of home life that friend has, because when your child goes over to spend the night or to a bunking party, their friend may have the kind of parents who let their kids stay up all night watching x-rated movies or listening to music they don't need to be listening to.

There are parents of teenagers who bring in liquor for them to drink or pot for them to smoke. You need to know the home life of the friend your child is running with and that's hard work. It's hard to stay up at night and wait for them to come in so you will not only know what time they come in, but what condition they come in.

I have a son who was born in 1943 and I heard him tell a friend recently that he lived at home until he was 20 years old. "I don't ever remember a night that I came in that my mother wasn't waiting up for me to kiss me good night."

The friend said, "Well, wasn't that sweet!"

"Sweet nothing! She wanted to smell my breath!"

Because my folks disciplined me, they laid down rules and they demanded respect. I understand a God who laid down rules. Who gave commandments and then said, "Keep them."

Wink-um

I WAS ABOUT 14 YEARS OLD and was going to a Sunday school party. Back in my days, that was just about the only fun in life. The only recreation that we had in that day was going to Sunday school parties and we had one every Saturday night in someone's home.

This particular Saturday night, I was going just across the street to Marian Parker's home. Daddy stopped me before going out the door and said, "Honey, wait just a minute. I want to ask you something."

"Yes, sir?"

"Darling, I understand that at your Sunday school parties you are playing some kind of 'goin' walking' game."

"Uh, I don't know what you're talking about, Daddy."

"I don't either. But, I understand the little boys and girls pair up and walk around the block."

"No sir! No sir! We don't do that."

He said, "I don't want you to. You're a good girl and I trust you. But those little boys aren't as big as you are. There is no way a little boy like that could protect you if some guy drove up in a car and decided to drag you into the car and drive off with you…he couldn't stop it. So, I don't want you out there on the streets. It's dangerous."

"Oh, no, Daddy. I wouldn't think about doing a thing like that."

I walked out of my house, across the street, into Marion's home and they were playing "wink-um." If you haven't ever played wink-um, you get all the chairs and put them in a big circle in the middle of the room. Stand all of the boys behind every one of the chairs and the girls sit down in the chair but there is one chair that is empty with no girl sitting there. The boy behind that chair looks around the room until he finds a girl that he wants to sit in his chair and he winks at her real big. She's supposed to jump up and run and sit in his chair. But, if the boy standing behind her can reach out and slap her on the head quick enough she has to sit back down in his chair. If she gets slapped on the head three times by the same boy they get to go walking around the block. That was our favorite game and we played it all the time.

This night I happened to be sitting in the chair of Fred Smith. Fred Smith was the "Fonz" of First Church. He was the first boy who ever had a motorcycle and a black leather jacket and every girl in the church had a crush on him. I was sitting in his chair. I managed to be slow enough to be slapped on the head three times and I got to get up and go walking with Fred. We walked out the front door to the end of the walk. We made a right and went down to the first corner. We made a right and guess who was sitting in their car around that corner? You see, that's why you can't let kids do anything they want to do. They don't have any *sense*. Why, if I had had any sense I would have known that all my mama and daddy had to do was look out the window. I wasn't across town. I was across the street. They were looking out the window and knew all these other kids were going around the block. They knew I had lied to them so it was just natural that I would be going around pretty soon too. And there they sat. I wanted to die. It's the only time in my life I just wanted the sidewalk to open up and swallow me. Daddy said, "Fred, go back to the party. Jane, we're going home."

I fell in that car, squalling and crying on Mama's shoulder, and she was petting me. Not one time did she say that Daddy was mean to do this to me but she was petting me and loving me. I said, "I'm not going to Sunday School in the morning! They'll be laughing at me."

Daddy said, "Yep, you're going to Sunday School in the morning."

"I'm not going to school Monday! They'll be laughing at me."

Daddy said, "Yep, you're going to school Monday."

We walked in the house and he said, "Darlin', I'm not going to punish you anymore tonight. I think you've probably had as much punishment as you need. But, there are three things that I want to tell you. In the first place, you lied to me and your mama and it nearly broke our heart. To think that you would look us in the face and bald-face lie. In the second place, it *is* dangerous out there. I could have been some pervert sitting out there and that little boy could not have stopped me from dragging you in the car. It is dangerous out there on the street at night for little boys and girls to be out. The third point I want to make, and I want you to remember this: From this night on, as long as me and your mama are alive, you will never know what corner we might be sitting around."

And I'll have you know that from that day until when they died in their 80s, I never lost that feeling. Any time I was tempted to do something that I knew I shouldn't do, I would stop and say, "Uh, oh, they might be sitting around that corner."

So, you see, I understand a God who says, "Jane, I see you and know exactly what you're doing."

You say that's fear. You better believe that's fear. But do you know that there is such a thing as healthy fear? That kept me from doing things that I wanted to do. I was tempted like anyone else was and I had lots of friends who smoked and drank in those days and every time they tried to talk me in to lighting a cigarette or taking a drink of whiskey, I thought, "Better not. Mama and Daddy will come around the corner."

Because of that I never smoked a cigarette or took a drink of whiskey and today I'm a strong Senior Citizen, able to travel and enjoy my grandchildren when many of those friends have long since died with lung cancer or live as alcoholics. So you see I understand a God who says, "The fear of the Lord is the beginning of wisdom."

Daddy

I TALK A LOT ABOUT DADDY because he was a partner with my mother in raising me. They were a team and did not work against each other. And I knew that I could not play one against the other. Daddy was very strict—not because he was mean, but because he was afraid something might happen to me. Mother was my advocate. She would explain to Daddy why he should let me do something that he had said "no" to—often changing his mind. But she never went behind his back and let me do something.

The only sport I ever learned to do was skate. I could not swim, ride a bike, or play ball. But, I could skate and loved it. When I was 14 a new skating rink opened in town. But Daddy would not let me go unless Mother took me and stayed with me while I skated. Several nights a week, Mother would take me and my best girl friend, Dorothy Mae, to ElCoNel Skating Rink to let me enjoy the one sport I could do. She would sit on those wooden bleachers for hours. I never wanted to leave until it closed. She was willing to sacrifice her time and comfort for my pleasure. Oh, what motherly love!

They were always ready to listen to me when I was ready to talk. No matter what they were doing, they would lay it down, sit down, and listen to my problems. I don't care how silly they were or how many times I talked to them about it, they would always take the time to listen to me. Therefore, I understand a God who can listen to all my burdens. He is always available.

Another lesson that Mother taught me was through another Sunday School party we had. We had a party every year on Sadie Hawkins Day. You dress like Lil' Abner, Daisy Mae, or Mammy or Pappy Yocum and the girls got to invite the boys.

I was about 14 and there was a boy named Joe that I was struck on but he wouldn't pay a bit of attention to me. I told my friend Laura that I was going to ask Joe to be my date for the Sadie Hawkins Day. Dates consisted of your mama dropping you off at the party and you sat and ate with them and that was as much of a date as it was.

Laura said that was fine. Three days later she came running up to me and said, "Goody, goody. I've asked Joe and he's going to be my date."

It nearly broke my heart. She was one of my best girlfriends and she had gone behind my back and asked Joe to be her date. I went home just squalling and I said, "I hate her. I hate her. I'm not going to ever do anything but hate her the rest of my life."

My mother said, "Now, wait just a minute, darling. You know the Bible says that if God is going to forgive you, you have to forgive others. You're going to have to forgive Laura."

"Mother, I can't do it. It was terrible."

"Yes, it was terrible but you've got to forgive Laura. We better pray about this."

So she got me down and we prayed about it.

"O.K., Mama. I'll forgive her but I'll not have anything else to do with her again. Not going to invite her to bunking parties. Not going to eat lunch with her at school. As far as I'm concerned, she has had it!"

"Darling, do you want God to treat you that way? Do you want Him to say, 'Jane, I forgive you for that but don't you ever come back to me again. I'm not ever going to talk with you or walk with you. I won't have anything else to do with you.'"

"Why, no."

"Well, maybe we better pray over this a little bit."

So, we prayed over it and I said, "All right, Mother, I'm going to be sweet and nice but I'm not going to ask any other boy because there's not anyone else I want to be my date. I'll just go by myself."

I went to that party in my little red and white polka dot Daisy Mae dress. Laura and Joe were there and I told her how pretty she looked. I told Joe how cute he looked in his Lil' Abner outfit and about that time the door opened and in walked a new boy who had just moved to Little Rock from Texarkana. He had been invited to that party and it was absolutely puppy love at first sight for the both of us.

We were sweethearts up until the day I met my husband. We were sweethearts all through school and it thrilled me that Laura had taken Joe off my hands, which gave me a chance to be Roy's sweetheart.

Going Steady

MY FOLKS WOULD NOT ALLOW me to go steady. This was great because I got to have several boyfriends at the same time. Even though Roy was my #1 Sweetheart, I got to date other boys too. I'll admit I was always boy crazy from twelve years old. Kids are goofy to go steady so young. You can have a lot more fun dating different people. I was not willing to go steady until I met Ted. Then I forgot all the others.

Mother's Prayers

MY MOTHER WAS THE KIND OF WOMAN who prayed for everything. Parking spaces. We would go to town and she would pray, "Lord, you know I need a space in front of Dillard's. Would you please open one up?"

We'd go down the street and there wouldn't be a parking space until we got in front of Dillard's and a car would pull out. She would pull in and look at me and say, "Isn't God good?"

She also prayed for things like lost car keys. One day, Mother had to go sing on the radio for the church and we had torn up that house looking for the car keys she had misplaced. Finally, she said, "Honey, let's just stop a minute and pray over this."

"Mama, you lost your car keys. You don't pray and ask God for something like that. It's your fault."

"Wait just a minute," she said. "If you had lost your car keys and were running late to be on a program and I knew where they were, don't you think I would help you?"

"Why, of course."

"Honey, the Bible says that God loves me more than I love you and He knows where my car keys are. God, help me find my car keys!"

She walked in and opened a dresser drawer that we had not even thought about looking in and there were the car keys.

Therefore, I understand a God who is willing to help me with the smallest, most trivial thing in the world that I can pray for.

Obedience

THERE WERE A FEW TIMES that I messed up. I was a pretty good girl. Never got in serious trouble. Never did anything really to be in trouble with my folks, but sometimes I didn't do something I was supposed to.

One time I was supposed to get a school theme in for my end-of-the-year grade. I didn't do it. Mother had said, "Jane, you better go to the library and get those books and get to working." I just put it off and put it off to the very last minute and didn't have it.

Mother said, "Now, Jane. I told you what to do about that. It's your fault and just get out of this mess the best way you can."

The next thing I knew, she was going to the library and she was getting some books and she was helping me get my theme together. And I thought, "Isn't that just like God?"

You remember when Adam and Eve sinned and God got so angry. He wasn't just upset. The Bible says that He was *mad* and he threw them out of that Garden and then He turned around and came up with a solution that would save them.

That was the blood sacrifice. He loved them so much that though they had broken His heart, He provided a way out for them. The plan was this: That man would kill the perfect lamb, pour its blood on the altar, and with the blood, his sins would be washed away. That was the only way that sins could be forgiven throughout the entire Old Testament. Then He came up with an easier plan, for man at least. He allowed his Son Jesus to be crucified on the Cross to be our sacrificial lamb and His blood cleanses our sin.

Have you ever wondered why God, who created the entire universe, didn't snap His finger and build a Bethlehem Hilton right on the spot when Mary needed a place to go? No, God intended for Jesus to be born in a stable because that's where *lambs* are *supposed* to be born. From that day until now, the only way our sins are forgiven is through Jesus' blood.

Parents, if you don't understand anything else I've told you and if you don't teach your child but *one* principle of God, you teach them this one: They don't get multiple choice. New Age religion won't get it. The only provision God made for salvation is through the blood of Jesus. It doesn't matter how *sincere* they are about how they want to worship God. I've heard people say, "It doesn't matter how I worship God if I'm just *sincere*."

Jane's father and mother, Victor and Fannie Gray

It does matter because if it didn't, Cain would have been OK. You remember Cain brought the best wheat and corn that he had grown. He laid it on the altar of God. He didn't thumb his nose at that altar and say, "This is stupid. I'm not making a sacrifice." He believed in God but he didn't worship Him the way He told him to. The blood of Jesus is the only way the Bible tells us we get to the Father so get this principle across if you don't do anything else.

Grand Parents

As I told you, I was their only child but I gave them three grandchildren. I watched them love each one of these grandchildren as if they were the only one they had. Yet they never showed favoritism. Each one of my children today would tell you that they were the favorite child of my parents. I watched them love the grandchildren exactly the way they had loved me. Their only begotten child.

Therefore, I understand a God who loves me every bit as much as He did His only begotten Son. In fact, He's made me a joint heir with Jesus and I, too, will own the cattle on a thousand hills someday.

They were always interested in the smallest details of my life. My friends. School. Who I dated. My marriage. My career. Then, I watched them have the same keen interest in each of the three grandchildren. Details of their life. Then, I watched them have the same kind of interest in the five great-grandchildren that were born before they died. All the details of their lives. Four generations had not dulled this love and this interest.

Therefore, I understand a God who is just as interested in me today...in where I work, who I married...as He was in Abraham or David or Paul.

THEY DIDN'T JUST LOVE the grandchildren. They also disciplined them exactly the way they had me. Grandparents, you don't do that child a favor if you spoil them until they become a rotten-spoiled brat. You just make people not love them. Be careful to make them respect your authority as they had their parents. That's the way my parents were about the grandchildren. They taught total respect.

When my daddy was 80 years old, he had his last heart attack and ended up in the hospital in intensive care for two weeks. In intensive care, one can visit for only 10 minutes every four hours. This is the way that we lived those two weeks.

One day my daughter Janie, who was married and had one child, was there. It was her time to go in to see Daddy. She walked in and said, "Oh, Papaw! You haven't eaten a bite of your lunch."

"Oh, Janie. Nothing tastes good to me. I can't eat anything. The only thing that would taste good to me is my homemade ice cream."

Daddy could make the best homemade ice cream in the whole world and Janie was the only one who had mastered his recipe. He said, "Honey, why don't you go home and make some of my homemade ice cream and bring it back to me." She said, "Yes, sir." and walked out of the hospital.

Four hours later, she walked through the intensive care unit and passed the nurse's station carrying a No. 3 washtub. In that was a wooden bucket with the ice and the salt running out into this big tub. And inside of that, was a gallon and a half of my daddy's homemade ice cream. The head nurse said, "Where do you think you're taking that?"

"I'm taking it to my grandpa. He told me to."

"You know you can't do that!"

"You go tell him. I never said 'no' to that man in my life and I'm not about to on his deathbed."

They took that freezer of ice cream and put it in their deep freeze and fed it to him every time he asked for it. He lived long enough to eat that gallon and half of ice cream.

Later, someone said to her, "Janie, why did you even think they would allow you to do that in the intensive care unit?"

"It never crossed my mind that I couldn't do it because my grandpa told me to."

And do you know that's why we Christians have such an up and down Christian experience through the years. We don't just do what God tells us to do without questioning it.

We don't not do what He tell us to not do. And if we would just accept that, our Christian experience would be a lot smoother. So that has helped teach me that whatever God says to do, do it.

At the end of that two weeks, we were all gathered around Daddy's bed knowing the time was near. And all of a sudden, he just began reaching up to the ceiling with both hands. I thought the medicine had gotten to him and I said, "Daddy, Darling, what is the matter?"

He said, "Angels! Jane, don't you see the angels?"

And he drew his last breath.

Therefore, my daddy helped me understand the promises of God. Which tells me that I don't have to cross Jordan alone. That He will send His angels to take charge over me.

Popcorn Calls

AFTER DADDY DIED, I WAS CAREFUL to go see Mother every day. Sometimes, three and four times a day. She didn't live far from me and I would just pop in and out through the day sometimes no longer than to just say, "Mama, did you take your pills?" and "I love you," and leave.

She called these my popcorn calls and she said, "Oh, honey, I just love your little popcorn calls. I wait every day—two or three times a day—just knowing you'll pop in and see me."

But about every two weeks, I would call her and say, "Mama, make some hot cornbread. I'm coming to spend the night with you and we're going to have cornbread and sweet milk for supper." She would make that cornbread and I'd go in and eat that cornbread and sweet milk and we would watch her favorite TV shows. I would sit down and manicure her nails and comb her hair. I would sit at her feet and tell her how I loved her. What a wonderful mother she had been. I would listen to her talk. I would let her go back and tell me about the first time she saw Daddy and about the things in her life that had been so wonderful. She would tell me how much she loved me and what a wonderful daughter I had been.

One night she said to me, "Darling, I like your little popcorn calls. I just wait every day for them and don't ever stop that. But you just don't understand what it means to me...when you just stop the world and get off and you come in and sit at my feet and you talk to me. And, you let me talk to you. You don't know what it means to me."

I know God hears our arrow prayers. The ones you shoot up when the least little thing goes wrong. You say, "Oh, Jesus, help me." He's happy that His name is on our lips every time that anything goes wrong. He accepts that. But, I'm sure that He gets lonesome for us to just stop the world and get off and sit at His feet and tell him how we love Him. What He means to us. And to listen to Him and let Him talk to us.

There was never a time in my life that I did not know that if it were necessary, my Mother and Father would have laid down their life to save me. They would have run into a burning house or thrown themselves in front of a Mac truck to save my life. Why? Because they loved me. They made me. They would have chosen me and I was the apple of their eye.

Therefore, I understand a God who gave Himself in the form of Jesus to hang on a cross to save me. Why? Because He loves me. He *created* me. He *chose* me. And I am the *apple of His eye.*

CHAPTER 2

Granny Diffee

Grandmother Sarah Jane Diffee at the age of 105

PROVERBS 31

Granny Diffee

Spiritual giant of the family

THE GREATEST GIFT A MOTHER CAN GIVE her child—more than money, more than education, more than fame—is to be a Godly Christian woman and point that child to God.

I had several Godly women who influenced my life. At first, it was my sweet, sweet mother who taught me the principles of God through her example.

The principle of unconditional love—that God loved me regardless of who I was or what I did. He *loved* me.

The principle of obedience. He expected me to follow His commandments.

The principle of forgiveness. He would forgive me for anything I ever did if I would just ask Him to. But also, that I had to forgive other people for anything they did to me if He was going to forgive me.

The principle of the truth. Only through Jesus Christ do you go to Heaven.

My Aunt Agnes Diffee was the pastor of my church for 18 years and I watched her live in the kitchen what she preached from the pulpit. I had several other aunts who loved me special and let me see Jesus through them.

I had spiritual mothers who had no children but reached out to me with love and mentored me. If you are a woman who has no children, find some child to reach out to and love. It can be very important.

The godly woman I want to share about was my Grandmother Diffee. She is directly responsible for me lifting up the name of Jesus because she was totally responsible for the direction her family took in life.

She was born Sarah Jane Shuffield in Bismarck, Arkansas in 1866. She was one of six children. At 15, she was saved in a brush arbor revival and, to our knowledge, she was the only one of the six children who were ever saved. They affectionately referred to her as their fanatic religious sister because she took her salvation seriously and she never wavered.

At age 16, she married Joe Diffee. They moved to Caddo Gap, Arkansas where he had a large farm and ranch. They started raising cattle and children. They had four boys and four girls, and each of them were two years apart.

There was a family on the adjoining farm, with just a fence between, that also had four boys and four girls about the same age as the Diffee kids. They became best friends and playmates.

Grandpa Diffee also had another job as a manufacturer and salesman. He was required to travel across the nation to other states and often was gone weeks at a time—sometimes, even months. He hired men to run the ranch, but Granny stayed home and raised the children.

There were no modern conveniences. No plumbing. No electricity. No gas. Granny would take the clothes down to the creek bank and beat them out on a rock to wash them and hang them all over the trees and shrubs to dry. One time, she told me her life was easier than mine because she didn't have to juggle PTA and Little League and Cub Scouts and piano lessons like I did.

Since there was no church in the area, every Sunday she put those eight children in the back of a mule-drawn wagon and drove for miles to put them in church.

Mothers, I know that the Bible says that the fathers are to be the spiritual leader of the family. It's wonderful when they are. But, if they are not, it is up to us to pick up the reins and run with them. I would venture to say that there are many people in church who would not be there were it not for their mothers. It may be due to the father's work or just indifference, but as mothers, we can not allow our children to not be in church just because the father does not come with them.

One day, a Holiness preacher came through the area and held a brush arbor camp meeting and it was the first time Granny had ever heard Holiness preached. She got sanctified. She talked to the preacher about the fact that there was no church in their area. There were lots of bootleggers and lots of gambling but there was no church. She was worried about her children growing up in the ungodly atmosphere.

He told her about a Christian Holiness school that went from the first grade through college in Vilonia, Arkansas. It was run by a group called Nazarenes and he said it would be great if her children could attend there.

Granny started praying over it. When Grandpa came in off the road, she told him that's where she would like to move and raise them.

At the old Caddo Gap home:
Granny Diffee with Jane and her cousins Roy Alfred Parker, Joe Thomas Diffee,
Sarah Elizabeth Diffee, Johnnie Carolyn Diffee, and Eloise Diffee

Jane's maternal grandparents,
Sarah Jane and Joe Diffee

Uncle Roy and Aunt Agnes Diffee
(Jane's pastor for 18 years)

"Janie. This is where our farm is. We can't do that."

"You can keep the same men running it who run it when you're gone and I really feel that God is leading us to move. If we don't, our children are going to turn out to be bootleggers and gamblers like everybody here is and I cannot have that."

She kept praying and working on Grandpa until she finally convinced him to move across the state of Arkansas. Caddo Gap is about 50 miles west of Hot Springs. Vilonia is about 35 miles north of Little Rock. They traveled that distance with those eight children in 1908. My mother was eight years old and the baby girl was six. They put all eight of those children in the Nazarene school.

J.B. Chapman was the president. A.S. London was one of the professors. Years later, that school merged with other Holiness schools to form Bethany-Peniel in Oklahoma, which is now Southern Nazarene University.

Each child grew up and married someone from that school. Agnes White married Roy Diffee and she became one of the greatest women preachers the Nazarene movement has ever known. She pastored First Church of the Nazarene Little Rock for eighteen years and was heard every day of those eighteen years on the radio that was heard across the state.

My parents, Fannie and Victor Gray, also met at the Vilonia school. They gave their musical talents to the Lord and sang in the church. Daddy was a choir director and president of the Gospel Music Association.

Lora Gray met John Diffee and they raised their seven children in First Church of the Nazarene in Little Rock. They later moved to Bethany, Oklahoma so the children could be close to college. Out of that union alone came preachers and missionaries, district superintendents, music ministers, military chaplains, doctors, youth ministers, and teachers. Three of the Diffee children, Lillie, John, and Fannie, married three of the Gray children: Luther, Lora, and Victor. All the Diffee and Gray children married other students from the school and from those unions came college professors, lawyers, engineers, scientists, and business executives who helped build churches with their money.

Except for one child who died young, Granny's other seven children all lived to ripe old ages, into their late 70s, 80s, and even 90s. Today there are dozens and dozens of grandchildren and great-grandchildren who, with few exceptions, are active in church today. They aren't all Nazarenes but that's okay. They are still in good basic fundamental churches. They teach Bible studies, sing in the choir, serve on church boards, run Jesus booths in inner-cities, and have a beach ministry on the coast.

What about the family next door—the one that stayed in Caddo Gap? Only one of their eight children lived past 40 years old. All the others died young tragic deaths as alcoholics or in gambling fights. One was killed in a shoot-out on Main Street. The girl who was my mother's age was killed in a one-car accident because she was intoxicated. Few children were born into this family and the last time I checked, no one knew if any of them were still living.

That's why I say my grandmother is responsible for me being here today. If she had not followed God's direction, there is no telling where our family would have ended up.

What about Granny? She was widowed at the age of 57. Grandpa died in 1923. The children never let her live alone. She moved around from family to family and her children fought over who *got* to keep her, not who *had* to keep her. She would stay at one house for several months and one of her other children would show up and say, "You've had her long enough. It's my turn." They would pack her up and take her home with them. That's the way she was loved.

My earliest memories of her are when I would sit at her feet and she would tell me Bible stories about Jesus. As a teen, I ran home one day to tell her something bad I had heard about somebody. Granny said, "Now, honey, you haven't walked in her shoes. You don't know what you might have done in the same circumstances. Let's just stop right here and get down on our knees and pray for her."

That took all the fun out of running home and telling something. I finally just quit telling anything bad on anyone because Granny would always make me stop and pray for them. Granny's idea was, whether it was true or not, Christians didn't talk about other people. They just prayed for them.

Another bit of advice Granny gave me: "Jane, I want you to know that this world is just a dressing place for Eternity. You're only put here to get ready to go into Eternity. What kind of clothes you put on in this dressing room determines whether you go to Heaven or Hell.

"If you want to go to Heaven, your garment has got to be white as snow, washed in the blood of the Lamb of Jesus Christ. And you cannot have on a dirty petticoat. The rest of the world may not see it, but God does and He's not going to let you in Heaven with some hidden sin that's made your petticoat dirty. It's got to be washed in the blood of the Lamb also." Pretty good advice.

Granny prayed daily—out loud for every child, grandchild, and great-grandchild by name. She ended every prayer she ever prayed, "Oh, God, don't let a one in this family miss Heaven."

When you visited her, before you left, you had to kneel down beside her. She put her hand on your head and she prayed for you.

Granny was the one who taught my mother to be a godly mother. She also had a great influence on my children. Just one week before my daughter Vikki went home to Heaven, she was preparing to give a speech to the Christian Women's Club in Poplar Bluff, Missouri on the influence Granny had been in her life.

Granny was never seriously ill. She never spent one day in a hospital in her life. She had a great sense of humor. There was nothing depressing about her. She could laugh louder at a joke than anyone in the family and loved to hear them.

Granny was never senile. Her mind was sharper than ever the day she died. But she came down with pneumonia and she died in my arms in the same bed in which she had helped with my birth. She was 106 years old and her family adored her. Mothers, it pays to serve Jesus. Please be faithful to your children. Sacrifice whatever you have to do to keep them in a Christian atmosphere. No, it does not take a village but it does take a church to help you raise your children to serve God. They need a dedicated pastor. They need loving Sunday school teachers. They need Christian friends their own age to keep them from the pull the world is going to have on them. If you will be a godly mother and be faithful to raise your children for God, they will rise up and call you blessed—and you will be able to point them to the Throne of God.

P.S. When Granny was 70 years old, Aunt Agnes Diffee, my pastor, gave me a piece of prose and asked me to learn it to give on Mother's Day in honor of Granny. She would sit on the platform in her little black suit, white blouse, black tie at her neck, white orchid on her shoulder, and represent the mothers of the church. Aunt Agnes said, "Jane, your Granny is very old. At 70, she may not be here another Mother's Day. She sat in her black suit, white shirt, black tie, and orchid on her shoulder while I gave "Parable for Mothers" in her honor. Then, for the next 35 years, I gave it every Mother's Day in her honor while she sat on the platform in her black suit, white shirt, black tie, and orchid on her shoulder. Then I gave it as a eulogy at her funeral when she was a few weeks short of her 106th birthday.

Parable for Mother's Day
By Temple Bailey

THE YOUNG MOTHER sat her foot on the path of life. "Is the way long?" she asked. And her Guide said, "Yes, and the way is hard, and you will be old before you reach the end of it, but you will find that the end is better than the beginning."

But the young mother was happy. And she would not believe that anything could be better than these years.

So she played with her children and gathered flowers for them along the way. She bathed with them in the warm streams and life was good. The young mother cried, "Nothing will ever be lovelier than this."

Night came. The children shook with fear and cold. The mother drew them close and covered them with her mantel. The children said, "Oh, Mother, we are not afraid. For you are near and no harm can come." The mother said, "This is better than the brightness of day, for I have taught my children courage.

The next day there was a hill ahead and the children climbed and grew weary. The mother was weary, but at all times she said, "A little patience and we are there." The children climbed and when they reached the top they said, "We could not have made it without you, Mother." And that night when the mother lay down and looked up at the stars she said, "This is a better day than the last, for my children have learned fortitude in the face of hardness. Yesterday, I gave them courage. Today, I have given them strength."

The next day brought strange clouds which darkened the earth. Clouds of war and hate and evil. The children groped and stumbled, but the mother said, "Look up. Lift your eyes to the light." The children looked and saw beyond the clouds an everlasting glory. And it guided them and brought them beyond the darkness. That night, the mother said, "This is the best day of all, for I have shown my children God."

The days went by and the weeks and the months and the years. The mother grew old and she was little and bent but her children were tall and strong and walked with courage.

When the way was hard, they helped their mother and when the way was rough, they lifted her for she was as light as a feather.

One day, they came to a hill and beyond the hill was a shining road with golden gates flung wide. The Mother said, "This is the end of my journey, and now I know that the end is better than the beginning. For my children can walk alone and their children after them.

The children said, "Oh, Mother, you will always walk with us—even after you have gone through the gates."

And they stood and watched her as she went on alone. The gates closed after her. They said, "We cannot see her but she is with us still. She is more than a memory. She is a living presence."

Grandpa Gray

MY PATERNAL GRANDFATHER, Tom Gray, was a Nazarene preacher who traveled from church to church in the county. He built the Liberty Nazarene Church just outside Vilonia which is still a thriving church today. Grandpa also farmed; however, after he had a heat stroke, he could no longer farm, so he sold Watkins products from a horse-drawn buggy.

My father, Victor, had to take over the farm chores when he was just a teen. That is why he only completed the eighth grade in school.

Jane's paternal grandparents, Mary and Tom Gray

He had to farm for the family. My paternal grandmother, Mary Gray, was of the Naylor family and her father founded the town of Naylor, Arkansas. She and Grandpa had five children. The first boy died, then they had Fred, Lora, Victor, and Alleen. Alleen died at age 14. Fred served in France during WWI. Grandmother Gray died when I was six years old and later, Grandfather Gray married Theresa who took such good care of him and made him very happy. They were married for years before she died. Grandpa lived until he was in his 90s, sitting daily with his open Bible in his lap. That's how my children remember him. They said they didn't remember seeing him without his Bible in his lap and reading it. Oh, what a heritage!

CHAPTER 3

Overcoming Adversity

Jane at age nine

PSALM 3:5-6

Overcoming Adversity

A loving family sticks together

CHILD PSYCHOLOGISTS would probably say a child that had to attend seven different grammar schools in five years would be warped—at least become an introvert and shy. But for some reason, I was able to rise above the problem. I'm sure it was because I felt such unconditional love from my parents, grandparents, aunts, uncles, and cousins. And my church family. I was always grounded in the Lord and know that helped.

I never felt poor, even during the depression days, except in the 4th grade at Kramer School. I had decent clothes, (my Aunt Maidie, a wonderful seamstress, saw to that). But I had no friends and felt lonely and poor for the first time. I ate lunch every day sitting in an outdoor stairwell by myself. That is, until the school put on a program. I was chosen, along with two other 4th grade girls, to be a grapevine and skip rope across the stage. We were told to have our mothers take crepe paper and cover the ropes with green leaves and purple grapes to make them look like grapevines. Well, the other mothers did just that. But, my mother, being an artist, dressed me in a complete costume like I was a full bunch of grapes, painting grapes all over the costume and making big, beautiful, hand-painted leaves and grapevines. You get the picture. The teacher and everyone else had a fit over my costume. They put me out in front and let me be the center of attention. Of course, the ham came out in me and I really went all out showing off. After that, I had lots of friends and was not lonely anymore.

But the condition that should have made me an introvert were the nervous habits I had from the time I was between 12 and 15. I think they call it Tourette Syndrome I had a VERY severe case of it. Anything from jerking my head, blinking my eyes, and distorting my mouth. I'd go from one movement to another, twisting about.

I'd try to stop one movement and take up another. It nearly drove my mother crazy. They took me to doctors, even one in Memphis. None helped. I kept this up, even into the 10th grade. Though I had gotten to where I could control it better, I would wiggle my fingers and feet where it did not show. By the 11th grade, I had pretty well stopped it. But to this day, I have to fight it. I will not even allow myself to show my kids what I did for fear I would start it again. This should have affected my personality and caused me to be shy. But I guess I have a strong enough will, because it did not.

It did not keep me from having boy friends or girl friends or living a very outgoing life. It did keep me from being in a style show in the 10th grade after I had been picked as a model. I overheard the teacher say, "We can't use her. Look how she shakes her head." I was determined to make myself stop and I worked on it until I did. I'm sure my mother's prayers helped.

Lost Fortune

WE WERE NEVER A WEALTHY FAMILY—at least not in my life time. Dad only had an 8th grade education. He was a hard worker and was a successful automobile dealer in his last 40 years. There were some lean years. Especially during the Depression. He had a very good job with Sinclair Oil but lost it when the Depression hit. I was six years old and had just begun first grade at Centennial School. Uncle John also lost his job. He and Aunt Lora had four children at the time. Mother, Daddy, and I moved in with them in their big house in Park Hill in North Little Rock. I went to Park Hill School there in Grade 2B. Then we moved to Conway to live with Aunt Madie and Uncle Willie and their two children, Ray and Louise. I went to grade 2A there. All the time Daddy was trying to get a job, doing anything he could to make a few dollars.

Mother was not well at the time, had never worked, and was not physically able to. After a year of living with relatives we moved back to Little Rock and Daddy got a job selling cars for Schumacher-Bush Ford (later Rebasamen Ford on West Markham Street). We moved to an upstairs apartment on Louisiana Street. Mother was bedfast at this time and a teen-aged orphan girl from church, Ella Mae Acock, lived with us to take care of Mother and me. I went to the 3rd grade at Rightsell School. During this time, Mother went to the hospital for major surgery. Dr. Robert Eubanks saved her life with the help of the Lord. She was in the hospital for one full month.

Granny was living in California with my Aunt Hattie and Uncle Walter Parker. They had gone there during the Depression to find work. They brought Granny back to see Mother, as they did not think she would live. After the surgery she was in a coma for days, during which time she had a vision of going to Heaven, visiting Jesus, then coming back to earth. I'm sure it was an out-of-body experience. She later wrote a play about it and I played her part when we presented it to church to an overflow crowd of over 1,200 people. Many people were saved during the altar call.

While Mother was in the coma, my Daddy never left the room. He sat in a straight chair by her side day and night. He did not sleep and only ate if food was brought to him. He refused to leave the room. She finally woke and the doctor said she was going to make it. Daddy hit the cold marble floor like he'd been shot and slept for hours.

We then moved to the Oliver Boarding House in North Little Rock, owned by a family in our church. I went to grade 4B at Woodrow Wilson School. Then we moved to the Blount Boarding Home in Little Rock, also owned by a family in our church. I went to the 4A grade at Kramer School. By this time, Daddy had been promoted to Used Car Manager for the Ford dealership and we were able to move back into the same apartment we were living when the Depression hit. It was across the street from our church and from Uncle Roy and Aunt Agnes Diffee.

I returned to Centennial for 5th and 6th grade. And all our old friends and cousins. We lived there until after I married, when Mother and Daddy finally bought a home in Park Hill. They lived there for 35 years until Daddy died at the age of 80.

Daddy was very successful in his profession and was hired as a used car manager for Von White Pontiac and Balch Oldsmobile. He then operated his own agency "Vic Gray Used Cars" at 711 Broadway. After retirement, he continued to sell used cars for other dealers. He was said to be the best auto appraiser in Little Rock. He did well for a man with an 8th grade education and had college graduates working for him. He was from the old school where the man took care of his wife and daughter. Mother never worked and neither did I until ten years after I married. Though we were never wealthy, we never wanted for anything.

But we should have had the wealth of a DuPont or Rockefeller. My Grandfather Diffee held the first patent on granulated soap powder in the U.S. His mother had discovered if she boiled peach tree leaves in her wash, it would help bleach her clothes. He used that formula, invented the soap powder, and he and Granny went to Washington, D.C. and obtained the patent. It was named Sunshine Soap Powder. He then began to travel from his farm in Caddo Gap selling stock.

By the time all the seven children were married, he was building factories in other states. He took all seven children, their spouses, and children with him to Georgia, Texas, Colorado, and California. He would get the factories going and sell stock to the local people. He would rent a large home big enough for all the families to live in and hire a cook and housekeeper. The grown children would go out in town, selling stock and soap. He was the kingfish, giving all the orders and they would follow after he got that factory up and going. He would move on to another state, always settling in a small town. He said he would rather be a big fish in a little pond than a small fish in a big pond.

When he finally got as far as California, he planned to build his last factory there and keep it for the family to run and grow with. However, at age 64, he had kidney disease and died suddenly. The family who worshiped him was devastated and because he had always told them what to do without teaching them how to run the business, they were at a loss. The oldest son, Walter, who had worked closer with him than the others, panicked and sold the patent to a little known company named Proctor and Gamble. It is in their history book that the patent was bought from a man from Arkansas. That is where "Tide" detergent came from. And our family could have owned it.

We never knew how much Uncle Walter got from the patent. He gave a hundred dollars to each of the other children—enough to get them back to Arkansas. He divided the rest with Granny, keeping the largest portion for himself. Granny lived 40 years as a widow, always with her children. But she still had some money left when she died. She bought nice gifts for her four daughters whom she divided her time between. If she bought one a washing machine, she bought all four of them a washing machine, etc.

When Granny turned 100 years old she announced that she wanted to buy herself a new car for her birthday. She could not be talked out of it. Mother dressed her in her little black suit, white blouse, black ribbon at the neck, white gloves and went to Balch Oldsmobile. She picked out a Fawn-colored 88 Olds off the showroom floor. Mr. Fred Balch himself came out to visit with her and take a picture of her by the car. He said, "Mrs. Diffee, do you still drive?" She said, "Why, son, I never drove a day in my life." He said, "Then why are you buying yourself a car?" She said, "Now when I want to go to a camp meeting, they have to take me because I own the car."

And for the next six years, go to camp meetings she did. Vilonia and Beebe and anywhere else she heard of one. We took her to all-day singings and dinner on the ground. To revival meetings all over the state. And when they would ask her to pray, she would pray the Glory down. After she died I inherited the car and always felt her presence in it.

Her last ten years—from 95 to 106, she lived with my folks. She was a beautiful woman. Soft wavy white hair, beautiful skin, Mother kept her dressed up all the time. Her eyesight got dim but her hearing never did.

When she turned 105, a reporter from KARK-TV came to the house to interview her after the big party. There she sat in her little black suit, white blouse, black ribbon tie at her neck, white orchid on her shoulder. She kept him laughing with her humorous stories.

After the interview, mother took her to her room to rest. Daddy took the reporter into the kitchen for pie and coffee where Mother joined them. Daddy said, "I think it's wonderful that Mrs. Diffee lived to be 105. But I don't want to live that long. I want to die before I'm 105."

From the bedroom, Granny yelled in her strong voice, "Fannie, come here." Mother rushed in to see what she needed.

She said, "Will you tell Victor you just don't die 'til you die. There's not one thing I can do about it."

Daddy, who loved her as much as his own mother was so afraid she would think he was complaining about her living that long. He assured her over and over again that he did not mean it that way.

The soap business was not the only chance our family had of being very wealthy. While in California, Grandfather Diffee had bought property on what was called Signal Hill in the Hollywood area. He kept it for several months, decided he would probably never do anything with it and traded it to a man for a Model-T Ford so he could make a trip back to Arkansas.

It was not too long afterwards that they struck oil on the land and Signal Hill is now covered with oil wells, still pumping. The record book shows that it was traded by a man from Arkansas for a Model T. So we could have been millionaires twice.

When I would bemoan the fact to mother about losing that chance to be wealthy, she would always say, "Honey, we might not be the Christians we are today if we were millionaires."

Oh, what a wise mother I had!

Jane Gray Krutz

64

CHAPTER 4

Love and Marriage

Jane at age 15

Jane at age 16

Ted at age 23

I CORINTHIANS 13

Love and Marriage

Love never fails.

IN 1942, right after Pearl Harbor had been bombed and the war effort was really picking up, there was a camp right outside Little Rock called Camp Robinson. One of my cousins had been inducted and my aunt and my mother said we were going out to Camp Robinson to see Ray before he was sent out to fight a war.

I was 16 at the time. We went into the large recreation room and about 200 soldiers were there. My mother, aunt, and I were the only females in the room and, naturally, the soldiers were noticing me, the only girl.

My mother never saw a piano she didn't play. She went up on the empty stage and started playing while the soldiers gathered around to sing along. Someone said, "There's our singer down there. He sings with our camp orchestra."

I looked and standing next to the stage was this black-eyed, black-headed soldier. I said to myself, "That has got to be the prettiest thing I ever laid my eyes on."

When someone asked him to come up and sing, he shook his head "no." I motioned to him and said, "Soldier, get yourself up here and sing for us." (He said I'd been bossin' him ever since.)

My cousin Ray had already told me not to give my name or phone number to any of the boys because half of them were married and I would not know who was.

But, after Ted and I had been flirting with one another, Ray said I could give my name and phone number to him because he was single and from Blytheville, Arkansas and a nice boy. Ray did not know that I had already given it to him and he said he would call me for a date.

And he did. That was an answer to prayer because I had been praying every minute from the day I met him that he would call me and ask me for a date. I just knew this was the boy for me. I explained to him how to get to my house in west Little Rock. He came into town on the bus. He needed to get off at Markham and Main and walk up to 5th and Main and catch the #6 Streetcar. That's the way we got around Little Rock in those days—on street cars.

He said, "OK."

I dressed up as pretty as I knew how but he didn't show up. An hour went by and he didn't come. An hour and a half. By this time, I was nearly in tears. I told Mother, "Well, there goes that. He decided he didn't want to date me and he's not coming."

About that time, the phone rang. "Jane, this is Ted. I'm in the camp. I'm confined to camp tonight."

"I understand that. This is war. You can't do what you want to do. You have to do what they tell you to and I understand that."

Jane and Ted

"Tomorrow night, could we have a date and I'll have a buddy with a car. He can bring me into town in the car if you can get him a blind date."

"Oh, I can do that."

The next night, he showed up with his buddy in the car and I had the gal, Jean Morgan, for the blind date. We went out on our first date and it was love from that moment forward.

Ted had one of the most beautiful singing voices and he sang to me all evening. That was the icing on the cake. In fact, twenty years later, he was offered a contract by Al Hirt to sing with his orchestra at a big salary but he turned it down, as he would have had to travel all over the country and he did not want to leave his family to do that.

Ted and I started dating and the next year we married. We were married before he told me the reason he broke that first date. He had arrived in town on the bus and walked up the street to catch the street car. He had never seen one before or been on one and he was too scared to ride it. He saw the fire coming out of the top of the wire and he just knew he would be electrocuted if he rode on that street car. He was afraid if he told me this that I wouldn't date him anymore...because he was a country boy.

He asked me to marry him and I agreed to it, "Yes, we'll get married after the war and I've had a couple of years of college."

In January of 1943 he was sent off to Camp Claiborne, Louisiana. We couldn't stand the fact that we couldn't see each other every night and talk to each other every day. We were in love and there just wasn't any way we could handle not being together. Ted was a drill sergeant and was training a new company. He got word he would be going overseas with his company the last of March. We nearly died to think we would be separated, so he asked me to marry him before he left.

He got a two-week furlough in March so we could have a two-week honeymoon before he left. Of course, though my parents liked Ted and had agreed to our marriage later on, I had to do some tall talking to marry sooner.

However, talking them into it was not my only hurdle. I was a senior at Little Rock High School (later Little Rock Central) with over 2000 students. They had a strict rule that a student could not graduate if they were married. No one had ever broken that rule. If they found out you were married the day of graduation, you did not receive your diploma. The principal, John Larson, was not about to make an exception. My mother went to him and begged him. She knew I would marry Ted before he left even if I did not graduate. He said, "No, Mrs. Gray. If I let Jane marry and graduate, then it would open the door for everyone."

That did not stop Mother. She went to the Superintendent of Schools, Mr. Hall. He asked for my school records and studied them. I had always made good grades and had volunteered for several teachers and programs in the school. He said, "Mrs. Gray, you know this is war time. We are sending boys straight from school to the battlefield. Maybe we should bend the rules a little for our soldiers. Yes, she can have a church wedding as you have requested, take a two-week honeymoon and come back and finish her Senior year and graduate. I do ask you not to put her wedding picture in the newspaper until after graduation."

Needless to say, Mr. Larson was not happy about it but could not go against the superintendent. However, he took me out of the Senior play, in which I had the lead.

"Mama, college or no college, I'm not going to lose the man I love and I'm going to marry him. I just can't help it, Mama. We're going to get married."

Wedding Day—March 14, 1943

They finally agreed to it.

At 4:00 pm, on March 14, 1943, we had a big church wedding at First Church of the Nazarene in Little Rock. I was 17 and Ted was just three weeks away from turning 24.

Ted was raised out in the country. He was raised by a good family but they didn't go anywhere. They didn't go to church. They didn't go to town. Ted went to school. Ted worked the fields. Ted went to the grocery store. Ted went home and Ted dated girls, especially since he was voted the most handsome boy in his class. That was about the extent of what Ted had done.

Ted did not attend church until he met me. I couldn't date a boy who didn't go to church. That didn't mean just Sunday morning church. That meant Wednesday night prayer meetings, revival meetings, and all of that. He had already been through a revival meeting with Nettie Miller, gone to the altar, and was saved under her preaching.

But Ted had never seen a wedding.

He had never been to a big wedding or a little wedding. He missed the rehearsal on Saturday night because the train didn't get in until midnight. We had rehearsed late that Saturday night and his best friend who was in the army walked through it and told him, "Ted, I will tell you what to do."

Sister Diffee was my aunt, She married us and said, "Ted, don't worry about it. You'll just walk out with me and just stand there. I'll tell you when to turn around and meet Jane. I'll tell you what to say. There's not a thing to it."

He walked out and faced that crowd of 1,200 people. It was packed solid, folks standing around the walls, and the balcony was full.

My mother who was a beautiful musician and a wonderful artist, also directed all the pageants and programs at our church. Hollywood and New York missed it when they didn't get Fannie Gray because she could take a few Nazarenes and a few little props that she could get her hands on and put on a pageant that was equal to anything you've ever seen. With me being her only child, she was going to put on a wedding that people wouldn't forget.

I told her, "Mother, I'll pick the bridesmaids and Ted will pick the groomsmen and who is going to be in the wedding. I'll just turn the rest of it over to you and you plan it."

Well, she planned it.

She had violinists and organists and soloists and duets and trios singing from the balcony. The only reason she didn't have doves flying out of the baptistry is that she just didn't think about it. She put on the wedding of the century.

There poor Ted stood in front of the congregation, and the ceremony and processional lasted over an hour. That was in the days when we didn't have the sense to take the photos before the wedding so we waited until after the wedding and it took about an hour to photograph the six bridesmaids, groomsmen, junior bridesmaids, two flower girls, and ring bearers.

The reception was at our house just a block away and all 1200 people came and went through the line. By the time we went through the wedding and pictures and reception, it was already dark by the time I got dressed to leave for my honeymoon.

Of course, I had a going-away outfit, too. Back in those days, the brides dressed up to go away. I had on a blue suit with a pink lace blouse, a pink tam, and an orchid on my shoulder. Today, they leave in blue jeans and leather jackets. Back then, we dressed up to leave town.

With Mother being an artist, many brides who married out of the Nazarene church got a beautiful gown and negligee—called a peignoir set—on which Mother had hand-painted roses around the bottom and up the chiffon. She had done this for nearly every bride who had ever married in the church.

For her daughter, she had created a gown trousseau. Seven satin gowns and chiffon negligees in every color. White, pink, yellow, blue, purple, green, and black. Seven gowns to wear the first week of my honeymoon. She hand-painted a different flower on every one of them that would go with each color. She bought me seven pairs of new satin house slippers with ostrich plumes across the front. Each pair was dyed to match the colors of the gowns and she hand-painted on each one of those shoes. My gown trousseau was the talk of the town. That's what Mother had for me. Today, new brides wear oversized Mickey Mouse t-shirts for their honeymoon. But back then, we wore peignoir sets.

We left on our honeymoon. We had reservations at the Peabody Hotel in Memphis. At that time, Memphis was about three or three and a half hours away. There was not a freeway from Little Rock.

The Peabody Hotel was as famous then as it is now. It's famous for the ducks that walk out to the pond. That's where we were going to spend our honeymoon with all seven of those gown sets.

We set out and it was well into the evening—7 or 8 p.m. It was dark. We got about ten miles out of town and realized we had left the marriage license. In those days, they did not allow a serviceman to stay in a hotel with a woman unless he could prove that he was married to her. They even told us when we made the reservation to be sure and bring proof of marriage or we couldn't stay there. We had to turn around and go back to the house and get that marriage license. We started out on that three and a half hour trek and by this time, it was probably 9:00 p.m.

We got to Brinkley, Arkansas which was about half way in between Little Rock and Memphis. Brinkley was a little country town with one tourist court. There were no Holiday Inns. There were either large hotels in town or tourist courts out on the highway. We stopped at the Riceland Tourist Court.

Ted said, "Honey, I am so tired. I've been on my feet since 3:00 this afternoon. Would you mind if we stopped here to spend the night and then tomorrow we'll go on to Memphis to the Peabody?"

"Anything you want to do, Darling, is all right with me."

I didn't even know I could have said, "No, I want to go on to the Peabody." I thought that since he said we should stop that we should stop.

A 10x10 room. Linoleum on the floor. An iron bedstead. One little dresser. A nail on the wall to hang clothes on. That's where we spent the first night of our marriage. I was so happy that I thought I had just died and gone to Heaven because I was married to this man whom God had put across my pathway.

The next morning we got up and went downtown and there was one restaurant on Main Street. It looked like one of those restaurants you would see on a Norman Rockwell calendar. Pickup trucks were all parked out front and we parked our car out front with "Just Married" still all over it.

I walked in wearing my blue going-away suit with the pink blouse, tam, gloves, and orchid on my shoulder. No one was in there but farmers in bib overalls—drinking coffee and spitting tobacco juice. We sat at a table and ordered hot cakes.

"Ted, they're all looking at us. Do you think that they know that we just got married? I'm so embarrassed."

I don't know how they could have told but that's exactly how I felt. We ate our breakfast and out we started toward Memphis. I was so happy.

We were going to go to Memphis and spend two or three days there and then go to Blytheville to meet his folks. His folks didn't leave home. They had not come to the wedding so I had not met them. Blytheville was about two hours north of Memphis. We got to the Mississippi River bridge and Ted said, "Honey, I just don't think I can wait another two or three days for my family to meet you. Would you mind if we went to Blytheville first and I took you to Memphis later?"

"Anything you want, Darling, is all right with me."

I had no idea that I could have said, "No, I don't want to go to your home for my honeymoon. I want to go to the hotel."

So we turned north and went there. We drove through that little town of Blytheville—two miles to the other side—to a little white house with a screened-in front porch where Ted had been born and raised.

I met his parents and it was love at first sight. I had a wonderful relationship with my in-laws through the years. I loved his four older sisters. I am still very close to his nieces and nephews. They lived in a little farm house and that is where we spent the first week of our honeymoon. I loved every plank in the floor because I knew he had grown up on them.

There was a wood-burning cook stove in the kitchen, two bedrooms, and no inside facilities of any kind. The only facility they had was about twenty yards out the back. A path led through high grass to get to it. But I was so happy to be married to this man that I had no idea that I could have fussed about it or said anything against it.

Ted did tell me that he felt a little guilty when he looked every morning and saw me going through that tall grass with a different colored hand-painted gown and negligee. I don't think that's what Mother had in mind when she was painting them. But I was happy to be Mrs. Ted Krutz and I was not the least bit unhappy.

And do you know, that rascal never took me to the Peabody Hotel to spend the night. Now, he took me a couple of times to see the ducks in the pond but in 65 years I had yet to go to the Peabody Hotel. Every time we talked about going on our anniversary, he decided it might be a little too expensive and we would wait until next year.

After a week in Blytheville we returned to Little Rock for another week. I took Ted to school to show him off to all my teachers and friends. He was so pretty. No Hollywood star was better looking.

After his furlough he went back to Camp Claiburn to get ready to leave for overseas with his company. There was lots of crying. I went back to classes and Senior tests.

Then, lo and behold, the day he was to ship out, he called to say they had pulled him out from the group and said he would stay to train another new company. He was a good drill sergeant and they needed him there. He was able to come in May for my graduation. Over 600 students graduated and I left the next day with him for Alexandria, Louisiana. He had already found us a place to live—which was not easy.

Jane, Janie, Teddy, Vikki, and Ted Krutz in 1954

Alexandria was an average-size, almost small town with three Army bases and two Air Force bases. It was wall-to-wall soldiers and there were very few places to live. There was a little widow in the Nazarene Church who had turned her home into bedrooms for servicemen and their brides who came to her church. She gave us a place to live.

It was a converted upstairs porch that she had built walls around, put a divider down the middle, and made two bedrooms out of it. Besides the two who lived up there, she had three other couples living downstairs. She also lived there with her two grown children. There was one bathroom in the house and one kitchen. We shared that bath. We shared that kitchen. We each had a little spot in the refrigerator that we kept our food. We also shared the sink and the stove with these other five couples. Our bedroom still had clapboard on the wall. Our closet was a nail on the back of the door. The only air conditioning back then was an oscillating fan. There was air conditioning only in department stores, restaurants, and movie houses. None in the homes. Very few attic fans. I had a little oscillating fan but I was so happy that I wish I could be that happy again before I go to Heaven as I was in Louisiana.

You should try hot summers in Louisiana. They don't get any worse. Sticky and humid. There's nothing hotter than Louisiana in the summertime without air conditioning. By now, I was expecting our little Teddy Boy.

Teddy was born at the end of that first year on December 20, 1943 and we were lucky and got to stay another year. Ted would train companies to go overseas and we never knew if he would go with them. So we made the most of every moment. We didn't know when we kissed good-bye every morning if he might call that day and say he was going overseas. Needless to say—we never spoke an unkind word to each other during those two years.

Luckily we stayed there until Teddy's first birthday and Ted was discharged. We brought Teddy home to Little Rock. Ted didn't like being a farmer and didn't want to go back to the farm, so we stayed in Little Rock and he became a salesman.

Two daughters followed Teddy—Janie and Vikki. They were three years apart and we settled in for a good family life. We were never wealthy. Ted was a good salesman. I didn't go to work until after all the kids were in school, but I got a job as a building manager which let me spend lots of time with the children. It was okay that we didn't have much money. We budgeted well and we got by, but it was okay.

We were in love and had three good kids. They were all healthy and we did all the things we were supposed to do. We went to church and we worked in the PTA, the Scouts, and the Little League. The kids took piano lessons and they all grew up, made good grades, finished school, got married, and left home.

You might think, "Jane, you have had a perfect life. You married the man you loved. You had three healthy good kids. Therefore, you must have lived happily ever after." Don't you kid yourself.

Ted Krutz and I had so little in common that we should not have said "howdy do" on the street. In fact, we had nothing in common except for our love for each other. A love for our children. A love for our Lord. But, other than that, forget it!

We were like two mules, tying each of them at opposite ends of a wagon, and hollering "giddy-up." That's the way our life was because we were so opposite. I'm loud and an extrovert. Ted was rather shy and quiet, a timid introvert. I'm happy in a crowd of 300-400. He was uncomfortable in a crowd of thirty. I want to go to everything. If there is a flea circus, I want to be on the front row. He wanted to stay home and not go anywhere. I should have picked up on this when we were dating.

I would say, "Honey, what do you want to do?"

All the other boys I went out with wanted to go skating, have a picnic, or go to the zoo—always wanting to go somewhere.

Ted would say, "Oh, Darling, I'm so happy with you that I don't want to go anywhere. I'm happy just sitting in the living room looking at you."

I didn't know that was going to be his way of life. That he would never want to do anything but sit in the living room and look at me. Even so, He went with me to parties and programs. He had a wonderful, cute personality and would often entertain with his guitar and beautiful singing. Everyone loved him and he was often the life of the party.

I like to travel and go to exotic, faraway places. I like to go visit all my cousins all over the U.S. He didn't like to travel at all. The only place Ted liked to go without fussing was to see the kids and that couldn't be too often because you had to leave home to do it.

I loved the theater. I loved to go to symphonies, the Rep, and to Broadway shows. His idea of big time entertainment was sitting at home in front of the television watching "Nashville Now" or World War II re-runs.

I loved to go to fine restaurants where they burn candles and lay the napkin in your lap. His idea of eating out was where there was a two-for-one coupon.

I loved to belong to all the clubs and auxiliaries I could join and any volunteer effort I could do. I would join anything if it was a good cause. Ted said that if they bragged on me, I would join it. He didn't want to go anywhere but to church. He would go there and maybe, once a year, to an American Legion meeting.

Our eating habits aren't even the same. You can tell if you see me that I have a problem with eating. I have three sets of clothes at home because I never know what size I'm going to be. I suffer from gluttony and vanity. I'm too big a glutton to stop eating and I'm too vain to be happy fat, so I'm at war with it all the time.

Ted could still wear his World War II uniform. He didn't eat anything if it wasn't good for him.

We couldn't even shop for groceries together. I went in the grocery store with a list and grabbed things off the shelves and threw them in the basket. Ted read every label on every bottle. It took him two hours to buy three things. He read even where it was manufactured.

But I don't mean that kind of trouble. I'm talking about heart-break trouble that sometimes comes into a marriage.

Our son Teddy was 20 when he met a beautiful girl in another denomination. She was a lovely girl and they had a big church wedding. A year later, they had our first grandchild, Kyle. We settled in to enjoy that grandson. Six months later, they were divorced. It devastated me. There had never been a divorce in my family on either side as far back as records are kept in the State of Arkansas. And my first child was divorced with a baby. His wife remarried and moved off to another city. She took that little boy and we didn't see him often during his years of growing up.

Teddy remarried and had another son, Jon. They divorced and his ex-wife remarried and moved out of state and we also did not see Jon often as he grew up. We are now very close to both boys and their families.

Both of the girls married and had big church weddings in our church. We settled in again for a happy family life.

Janie is our middle child, the oldest daughter. She had dated her boyfriend seven years through high school and part of college when they married in this big church wedding. They didn't have any children but two years later, she walked in and informed me, "I'm filing for divorce."

I was embarrassed. All my cousins' kids were married and doing well and mine were getting divorces one right after the other. I was angry at her because she was the one wanting the divorce. Her husband didn't want one. We felt like we had raised him because they had dated so long. Both sets of in-laws were devastated. I loved her husband and her in-laws loved her. I was mad at her and wanted to tie her to a bedpost.

However, being a good mama, I shut my mouth. She got the divorce and we loved her through it. If your children are going through this, be sure and know what the problem is. You should try to work out the marriage but sometimes you can't.

Janie met an Air Force Captain in Little Rock and fell madly in love with him. They married and a year later, we had our third grandson, little Victor. Three months later, our Vikki had a little girl, Jennifer, so once again we settled in to enjoy these two grandbabies.

A few weeks later my husband, Ted, whom I had been married to for thirty years, came in from off the road one day and said, "Jane, I'm not happy. I've been thinking about it for a long time and I think we need a trial separation to see if this marriage needs to be kept together."

I could have died. I could have buried that man easier than hearing that from him. This was the man I had loved for thirty years, had born three children for, and he wasn't happy? I wanted to throw my arms around his ankles and say, "No, you aren't going anywhere."

But I thought, if he really wants to and I make him stay, what good has it done me? Maybe I should let him go, pray over it, and see if the Lord could work this thing out.

"Go on and go if that's how you feel about it."

I was so hurt and angry. I filed for a divorce. Ted begged me not to. He only wanted a trial separation. I said, "No, Brother, you're getting more than you asked for."

When he moved his personal belongings out of the house, I fell on the floor and screamed. I kicked and beat my fists on the floor until they bled. I screamed so loud that if the neighbors had been home they would have called the police. That's how bad I hurt.

I went around like a zombie. I went to work. I tried to go to church. I did not understand why the church was the hardest place for me to go. I would go in and start crying and have to leave. I would go in and sit in the service and it was like a black cloud was over me. I could go to work and stay busy, but it was hard to go to church. Sometimes I would get into the vestibule and start crying and have to leave. It devastated me totally when the separation happened.

Three months later, our daughter Vikki's husband asked for a divorce. I moved her and her three-month-old baby girl in with me.

Three months later, Janie's husband the Air Force Captain, whom she worshiped and adored, was killed in a C-130 Air Force accident. I moved her and her nine-month-old baby boy in with me. And there I was, a middle-aged divorced woman with two daughters. One, curled up in a fetal position with a nervous breakdown because her husband had been killed. The other one, bawling her eyes out because of the divorce.

I would go to work through the day and come in at night and rock two crying babies on my lap. You think I didn't feel "rained on"?

I never blamed God. I never said, "This is God's fault. Why did you do this to me?"

But I did ask Him, "Why did it happen?" And I reminded Him that He had asked "why" on the cross. I cried out to Him. I would go to the church altar during the day when no one was there except the secretary and the janitor and I would cry and pray and ask for help. I was drowning in my troubles. I felt like I was going under for the third time. I never once thought about suicide but I did understand for the first time why some people try it.

Chuck Millhuff came to First Church of the Nazarene Little Rock for a revival and I had to force myself to go to the meeting. One night he preached on the simple little story about the boat that was out in the storm. Jesus was preaching on the Sea of Galilee. He was preaching to the disciples and He said to the disciples that they should get in the boat and go across to the other side. He went to sleep in the boat. The storm came. The water came and the winds blew. The disciples were frightened and woke Jesus up. "What's the matter with you? Are you going to just let us drown? Don't you even care if we die in the storm?"

"Oh, ye, of little faith."

He stood up and said, "Peace. Be still." The storm was stopped. My mother has painted portraits of that very scene.

Chuck Millhuff said that wasn't the big miracle in all of this. Storms had come and gone throughout the ages, but it is the only place in recorded history that says the boat was filled with water—but not one word about it going under.

I think that's why Jesus said, "Oh, ye, of little faith." As if to say, "Didn't you know that I was in this boat with you? Did you think I was going under? Didn't I tell you that we were going across to the other side?"

At that moment, I was aware of the fact that I had Jesus in my boat! That if I didn't jump out, we were going to stay together and get across to the other side. My spirits began to rise.

Right after this revival, Rev. Gary Haines came to Little Rock. He held a one-week revival at Central Nazarene Church, followed by one week at North Little Rock Nazarene Church. I went to every service. Gary did not know me or anything about me, but every sermon was for me and my problems. During those two weeks, I really settled it with the Lord. Gary and I became very close. He is my adopted Preacher Boy and I am his adopted second mom. I flew to Colorado to see him receive his Doctoral degree.

Ted soon came back wanting to come home. He told me how sorry he was. That the devil had made him have these thoughts that things weren't as wonderful at home as they ought to be. He cried and begged me to take him back.

My first impulse was to throw my arms around him and say, "This is what I've been praying for." But it seemed like the Lord said, "Wait, Jane. Just give it a little bit of time. Be sure this is what Ted wants to do. Pray about it. Counsel about it before you totally go back together again." That's what I told Ted we were going to have to do. We sought counseling and went to the minister. We prayed over it together. I told Ted that I didn't want to be hurt again. I was getting to where I could breathe again.

I didn't let him move home and I didn't move in with him but we started dating. In fact, he took me to a restaurant or two that didn't even have coupons. He would come at night and baby-sit with me. We kept the two babies because the girls had gotten to where they could get up and get out some at night.

We were sitting there one night. He had Victor on one knee and I had Jennifer. We were rocking in the den and I said, "Honey, what happened to us? We were the perfect "Father Knows Best" kind of marriage and home."

"Yes. But don't you think in our case, Jane, that it might have been called "Mother Knows Best"?

Yes, I am heavy-handed and opinionated. I'm a strong and take-hold, in-charge kind of person. I prayed about it and the Lord showed me that I had not given Ted his proper place in the home that I should have. I had made him feel inferior because of my leadership. I was proud of my profession and was doing well as a building manager.

I had not read Titus 2 as I should have. It tells us that we are to let the husband be the leader of the home. I hadn't done that and the Lord really dealt with me over it. I struggled over it. I laid on my face at the altar and prayed over it. I gave up some things in my life that had taken priority where they shouldn't have.

I prayed and I prayed and I prayed until I knew that I knew that I knew that I was supposed to go back to Ted.

We went back together after a year and a half of separation on our 32nd wedding anniversary (March 14, 1975). Since neither of us had married anyone else, we were able to have the divorce annulled. That way, our marriage never had a break in it. We went into the preacher's office and said the marriage vows together because I wanted us to really commit to that. We talked it over and decided we would work together and compromise. I would give up things and he would give up things. The truth was, he gave in a little and I gave in a lot and we compromised and worked on the things that had caused the trouble.

I gave up clubs I belonged to—especially anything where I went out at night to a meeting and he was left at home. I agreed to go to restaurants where coupons were good. He agreed to go on vacations if we didn't go on too many of them.

A few months after we got together, we got in a fuss over something (I would be lying if I said we didn't have a cross word after that because we were too different to not disagree on some things).

Ted said, "Jane, do you think we need to separate again?"

"No, Boaz. Ruth is here until the end of the harvest. I'm not going anywhere. You're not going anywhere. We agreed that we would commit to this marriage and nothing short of physical violence, we will not separate."

"Well, if that's your attitude, we might as well quit fussing."

We fussed a little bit after that but not the way we used to, because we knew that fussing was not going to separate us. We were not going anywhere. We were committed. We didn't have the option to split up. That was the agreement we had. We would struggle through whatever misunderstanding we had.

That's my advice to married couples—whether young or old. Commit that you're not going to have the option to split. If you don't make that commitment, every time he does something you don't like, you'll say, "I'm going home to Mama."

And every time she does something you don't like, you'll say, "I'm walking out. I'm not putting up with this anymore." And you'll constantly have an up and down marriage. Commit that you are staying through the marriage—that you are going to stay together.

It takes two to stay married and sometimes that doesn't happen. As long as you keep Jesus in your marriage boat, you'll go across to the other side with that type of commitment. I can truthfully say that the last years of our marriage were the best years. They were the sweetest years. They were the years that had no fight left in the marriage. He told me every day he loved me and how happy he was that we were still together.

That is the way a good Christian experience should be. That's what we Nazarenes call sanctification. It's when you make that commitment that "I'm here to stay. I'm not going anywhere. I'm here with Jesus until we go across to the other side. I'm not going to let the devil tempt me to do things I'm not supposed to do." If you don't, every time a temptation comes along, you might say, "Well, God might not have really meant that I wasn't supposed to do that. Or, God didn't really mean that I have to do that."

It's a constant up and down fight in your Christian experience. If you will make a commitment to your Christian experience that it doesn't matter what comes or what goes, you're in that boat with Jesus until you go across.

Do you know that in several places in the Bible, Jesus likened our Christian experience with Him to a marriage. He knew we could understand it better. He said that He is the bridegroom and we are the bride. It's just like a marriage. He comes courting us through the Holy Spirit and He woos us to Himself. He asks us to marry Him and that's what we do when we are born again.

We accept that proposal. We marry Jesus Christ. We become His bride. We take on His name as a Christian. I took on the name of Krutz when I married Ted. We drop all the other suitors and all the other people who have been running after us for our attention. We drop them. We drop friends who won't fit into our marriage with Jesus. He moves in with us. He's our constant companion just the way my husband should be my constant companion in life.

He loves me. He comforts me. He guides and advises me the way a bridegroom should. He also does what bridegrooms do. He is building a home for me to live in with Him. In fact, it's a mansion. He has promised that when He has finished that mansion for me, He is going to come back and get me—all of us who are His bride. He's going to come and pick us up. He's going to carry us across the threshold of Heaven. He's going to sit us down at the marriage supper of the Lamb. We will live with Him forever as His bride.

I don't aim to miss it. How about you?

P.S. Each one of the children found true love in another marriage. Teddy and his wonderful wife Debbie live in Destin, Florida.

Janie was a widow for ten years and then married Dr. George Lay, an orthodontist in Heber Springs, Arkansas. He adopted 11-year-old Victor and then he and Janie had a little girl, Sarah Jane. Vikki married Pat Kreulen, who helped her raise Jennifer, and they had two wonderful boys, Jake and Ben. Pat became a nurse practitioner and took such good care of Vikki through her long illness with lung disease. She had a double lung transplant but, after one and a half years, died at the age of 51. I questioned why God would take her to Heaven when she was winning souls for Him here on earth all the time. She led a 16-year-old girl to the Lord on the Walmart parking lot just one week before she died. I told the Lord she would do Him a lot more good here than in Heaven. My pastor, Dr. Dan Casey, said, "Maybe Vikki had lived so close to the Lord and done so much for Him, she deserved to see Jesus before us."

After 64½ years of marriage, Ted went home to Heaven at the age of 88. Still beautiful, his last word as he looked up at the ceiling was "Vikki!" I knew she was there waiting for him.

I've been able to stay in our home for over 50 years with the aid of an electric chair on the stairs, due to my arthritis. I can still drive at 85, even at night. I still give speeches and appear on AETN fundraisers although I'm sometimes using a walker and have to sit on a stool.

There is still a 16-year-old floating around in me who just will not give up. I can hurt going places as well as hurt at home—so I keep going.

I'm very close to my children and grandchildren. We have lots of fun together, talking every day on the phone and seeing each other often.

I'm also very close to all my many cousins—ten of them are double cousins. I feel as if they are my brothers and sisters. We visit often.

At my 85th birthday party, hosted by AETN, I told the crowd that I had lived a charmed life.

I had won the Parent lottery with parents who loved me unconditionally and taught me to respect authority with strict discipline.

I had married the man I loved and had three wonderful children, seven grandchildren, and six great-grandchildren.

I want my kids to know that there are a couple of things in this life that really pay off. The first is serving Jesus. The second is serving others through volunteering.

Teddy, Vikki, Janie, Jane, and Ted in 1951

Janie, Vikki, and Teddy in 1952

Vikki, Janie, and Teddy in 1967

Janie, Teddy, and Vikki
at Camp Polk, Louisiana

Vikki crowned as Miss UALR 1970

Vikki, Ted, and Janie sing "What a Day That Will Be."

Janie, Teddy, and Vikki

Jane and Ted with America's Junior Miss Julie Forshee

Vikki

Jane and Vikki

Jane and Janie

Janie—always full of laughter

Jane and Ted at one of Jane's speaking engagements.

50th Anniversary Celebration
March 14, 1993

Jane and Ted in the back yard

Ted and Jane on a cruise ship.

Jane and Ted at the Waldorf Astoria
in New York City

Jane and Teddy at Jane's 85th birthday party—September 30, 2010

Royalty

ONE OF MY CALIFORNIA COUSINS, Sherri Jones, worked on our Gray genealogy and found out we really come from royalty. That information and $1.95 will get you a cup of coffee almost anywhere, except Starbucks®.

It turns out that our Great-Grandmother, 17 times removed, was Queen Elizabeth of England.

She had two sons. The one named Thomas is the line from which we come. But we can't brag too much. Queen Elizabeth's other son was Henry the 8th. 'Nuff said.

Jane and Dr. Gary Haines at his doctoral ceremony in Colorado Springs in 1997.

*Jane and Ted all dressed up
for an evening out.*

*Ted and Jane at Tom and Wannie
Longfellow's Christmas party.*

Teddy and wife Debbie

Jane Gray Krutz

CHAPTER 5

Success

Jane at the 1515 Building in Little Rock in 1963

PROVERBS 16:3

Climbing the Ladder

Steps to a successful career

PEOPLE ARE LIKE TEABAGS. You don't know how strong they are until you put them in hot water! Have you ever asked yourself where you would be today if it were not for the hot water in your life? I would probably be a very comfortable wife and grandmother. I would have a few friends in the church. I would do volunteer work but, other than that, I would be leading a very ordinary life.

I married at 17 and was a WWII bride. We had three children and I settled down to do exactly what I had always wanted to do. That was to be a wife and a mother.

I was the kind of mother who was the PTA President and a Cub Scout leader. I taught Sunday school and did a lot of volunteer work. I carried the kids to piano lessons and Little League practice and I was doing exactly what I wanted to do with my life. That lasted for about ten years. Then, I fell into hot water. The hot water vat of financial trouble. Have you ever been there?

The economy had gotten worse. One ordinary salary just would not cut it and I *had* to go to work. I was not prepared for this. I had married just out of high school. I only had a high school education. I had never worked a day in my life and had no desire to work. I was a totally fulfilled woman.

But this hot water pot that I was put in to forced me to make the decision of either working or taking the kids out of piano lessons and Little League and Cub Scouts and all of these little extras I wanted the children to have. I took a part-time temporary job. I wasn't going to work forever but just until we got a few of the bills paid. I was a bookkeeper in a small plumbing supply firm.

Now, I was really in hot water. Me? A bookkeeper? I couldn't even balance my own checkbook! I counted on my fingers. I hated detail work. I still do. If I can't do it walking and talking, I don't like it. I told my employer I was willing to work hard and learn how to do that job. I learned how and I came out of that hot pot—not a happy bookkeeper, but an efficient one.

After a year there, I went to work in an employment agency where I could interview people and work with the public. I liked it a lot better but it was still part-time and still temporary. I wasn't going to work forever.

After three years there, the economy got worse. The kids got more expensive. The water got hotter and I had to go to work full-time.

I found a good-paying job in a large real estate firm as a bookkeeper. I had thought that because I had kept books in a one-man operation, I could keep books for one of the largest corporations in Little Rock. Wrong!

Let me tell you I was in hot water there that I couldn't even tread! But it made me stronger, because I learned two great lessons.

NUMBER ONE: I learned that every job is not for everybody. If you are miserable in your job, if you are doing something you hate to go to every day, if you are in a job you can't really do well or can't hack it, you need to get out of there. Look for a new job, because there is one out there for you if you'll just look for it.

NUMBER TWO: The lesson I learned that was especially good for me was that there are some people you can not work with. This was good for me. I loved everybody and everybody loved me. I got along with the obnoxious and unlovely people in my life. I did not think there was anyone I could not conquer and handle. In fact, those three years that I was at the employment agency, when those clients of mine would come in and say, "Mrs. Krutz, I just can't work for that old man. He's just so mean to me." I would say to them, "You can if you want to. All you've got to do is reach out with kindness and love and tenderness and, before long, you'll have him eating out of your hand. You can do it if you want to."

Then, I was placed under a female supervisor that I could not handle. She wasn't nice to any of the employees in the firm but she just plain didn't like me. She took every opportunity to embarrass me and put me down and bawl me out in front of all the clients and all the other employees.

I tried all those things which I had told those girls through the years to do. I was sweet to her. I bragged on how pretty she was. I brought her little gifts. I took her out to lunch. Didn't work. I remembered that Mother had told me there are some people who really like you better if you stand up to them. I stood up to that gal. I stood nose-to-nose and gave her back exactly what she gave me.

Didn't work. She still didn't like me.

After only three months there and nearly having a nervous breakdown, I walked into the big boss of the corporation and said, "Sir, I want to thank you for giving me the opportunity of working under someone that I can't conquer or handle. Because it has mellowed me. It has made me more compassionate and understanding of other people who have this problem. But the main thing it's done for me, is it has given me determination that if I am ever in the place of authority, I will be nice to the people under me."

I walked out of there and I went to work as the secretary to the sales manager and the full sales department in a local TV station.

You haven't been in hot water until you have tried to be a secretary to the full sales force in a big TV station and you have never even seen a shorthand book.

Remember, this was over fifty years ago and they did not have word processors and very few Dictaphones. They handed me a pencil, a flip-top notebook that had a line down the middle and said, "Take dictation." I told the man I didn't know how to take shorthand but that I would learn to take his dictation if he would give me a chance. And, I learned. I learned to take dictation in longhand which totally wiped out my penmanship and if you can read my writing today, it's forged.

I learned that secretaries do most of the work and those salesmen go home with the big paychecks. I learned that I didn't like being a secretary, sitting behind a desk eight hours a day. By now, I had learned that I would probably be working the rest of my life. As the kids got older, they got more expensive. It was going to take two paychecks forever and I better get out and find me a job that I could be happy in and do well.

After three years there, I did what I had been taught as a child to do when I really got into hot water. I called on the Lord about it. I prayed over it and I explained to Him that I had not wanted to work. I was a very fulfilled wife and mother and I wanted to stay home with my kids. I wasn't working just to buy fur coats and diamond rings. I was working because I had to. I was going to trust Him to help me find a job I could be happy and satisfied with. He just dropped the job managing the 1515 Building in my lap. He at least dropped the opportunity to know about it and go after it and go after it I did. The hot water vats I had been forced to swim in helped me get this job and to excel at it.

Because of the fact that I had to learn bookkeeping, had to learn secretarial skills, how to handle people—even unlovely people— has helped me be a property manager. Don't ever be afraid to learn something on a job you don't want to learn. Because when you leave, that's the one thing they can't take away from you the knowledge you've gained.

I started the job at the 1515 Building in hot water because 50 years ago, women were not allowed to manage a high-rise office building.

Only men did this. In fact, I pioneered the field for women in high-rise office building management in Little Rock. And I was the first woman hired by Bloomfill Builders, the national company that owned my building and also buildings all across the South. They were in at least eight states. They had no women building managers. Only men. And they didn't want one.

I begged and I clawed and I fought for that job. I promised that if they would just give me a chance they would not be sorry. They finally hired me to shut me up. I started it in hot water because they only gave me three months to try it. They said, "We'll put you on a three-month trial. If you can't do it, you must promise that you will go to the back office and be secretary and bookkeeper to the man we will put over the building."

I accepted those terms because I wanted the job so badly. I agreed to it and bowed my back and worked myself nearly to death. Some days, sixteen hours. Some weeks, seven days. I studied everything I could find on property management and leasing. I took a real estate course. I took everything I could to learn about that job.

I started with 30% occupancy and in less than three months, had 100% occupancy with a waiting list.

This was like hitting them up side the head with a two-by-four. I got their attention. Once you get their attention, it isn't so hard. They couldn't understand it because it was the only building they owned in the nation that was 100% full and I was their only woman building manager.

They called in all the men. From the Trademark Building in New Orleans. The Peachtree Buildings in Atlanta. Managers from Tennessee, Texas, Oklahoma, and Alabama. They brought them in to Memphis to the home office. They sat them down and told me, "We want you to stand up here and tell them how a *woman* did what they could not do." I did not much like the way they said "woman."

I put on my prettiest smile and my most dignified voice and I said, "Gentlemen, I do know that you understand that a woman has to work harder than a man and do a better job than a man to be noticed. Fortunately, that isn't hard. But I will be glad to tell you how to fill a building.

You fill a building exactly the same way you do anything that you want to be successful in. Whether you are selling a project. Whether you're trying to build a Rotary Club, or selling building materials or insurance. Whatever you are doing in life, this little blue print will take you to the top of the ladder if you are really trying." Here are the twelve steps:

1. Hard work.

YES, I KNOW THOSE ARE FOUR-LETTER WORDS but lazy just will not get it. You have to be willing to work hard, above and beyond the call of duty. Maybe even work longer hours than they pay you for. Throw away that clock. I would have not filled that building in three months if I had been a clock-watcher. Burn that midnight oil and don't ever be guilty of using the phrase, "But that's not my job description." There isn't one word in my contract as a building manager that mentions "unstopping commodes" but I've unstopped a few when my maintenance man was busy. I told my kids that if their boss tells them to do anything—I don't care what it is—as long as it's not illegal, immoral, or unethical, do it! If he says the floor is dirty, go hunt for a broom. Because if you learn to do lots of things in your company, you're going to be more valuable to them. And, the main thing is, you'll be noticed. Once you've been noticed, they'll give you opportunities to climb that ladder. The first rule is "work hard."

2. Know your product.

KNOW EVERYTHING there is to know about it...tangible or intangible. Read everything written on it. Look at every tape that has been made on it. Take every course offered about it. Go to every seminar they hold on it. The Bible tells us that we should study so we will have a ready answer for anyone who asks us about our faith. You should study to have a ready answer for your client who asks you a question about your product. If you don't have it then, you tell them you don't have that answer right now but by tomorrow morning at 8 a.m., you'll have the answer. If you have to, stay up all night to study to have the answer to it. Ring their phone at 8 a.m. and say, "Here's your answer." I'll guarantee you that you will get their business.

My husband sold toilet paper for a living. He was a good toilet paper salesman because he got to retire early. After he retired, whenever we went into someone's home to visit, or to a restaurant to eat, or to a service station to gas up, before that day was over, he would tell me what brand of toilet paper they use in their restroom. Yes, he would. Not only that, he would tell me the ply (the thickness), the number of squares to a roll, and probably what it's worth on today's market. I wanted to say, "Who cares?" but I just smiled at that pretty little man and said, "Well, isn't that interesting!" Girls, that's how you stay married for 64 years.

The point is this: you need to know your product so well that, years from now, it's still going to be in your head. Do your homework and do your study. Know your product.

3. Be a good communicator.

WHAT GOOD DOES IT DO YOU to know about something if you can't tell anyone about it? You won't be able to explain to the boss if you have an idea that can help the company save a lot of money. If you have people working under you, you will not be able to explain to them what you expect out of them. If you have a problem with communication skills, there are courses you can take to help yourself. The ability to communicate is a necessary tool for a successful climb up the ladder.

In 1981, I had the privilege of going to Washington, D.C. to the inauguration of President Ronald Reagan. I went with three other gals and we had fun. We dressed up in our finest and thought everyone knew we were there even though we were there with millions of people. The first morning, we had the honor of going to the Kennedy Center for a coffee where we were able to meet Nancy Reagan for the first time.

Across the street from the Kennedy Center were the Watergate Apartments. In 1981, the Watergate Apartments were still a big thing in the news so I said, "That's where we're going for lunch."

When we arrived, we walked into a huge vestibule and every woman in Washington had decided to do the same thing. They were literally nose-to-back, which means if you were short, your nose was in someone's backbone. We were in there like sardines. The other women said, "Let's go somewhere else and eat."

"Not going to do it. I'm going back to Arkansas and tell them I had lunch at the Watergate Apartments. We're staying."

We shuffled around for a while. Standing on one foot and then another. Then I heard someone from across the room yelling, "Jane! Jane Krutz!"

I looked and it was Vonette Bright. Her husband, Bill, founded Campus Crusade for Christ. She was frantic. "Please come here and help me!"

I elbowed myself through the crowd and there with her was Dale Evans—Roy Rogers' cute little wife. She was in her darling little cowgirl outfit—with her hat over her back, a bolero, skirt, and cowgirl boots. She was the cutest thing. Vonette said, "Jane, we need help. This is Dale Evans and she is about to die to go to the bathroom and we can't find it. Can you help us?"

They were both short people and they couldn't see over people's heads. I said, "Honey, I'll do my best."

I wormed my way through the crowd to the maître d'. I assumed he was the maître d'. He was the only man in the room and had on a black tuxedo at noon so I thought that was who he was. I came up to his backside. It was so crowded, I could not get in front of him so I jerked on his coat tail and said, "Sir, can you please help me?"

He drew himself up to his full 6'4" height, twisted his head around, looked down his nose at me, and said, "Madame, you will have to wait your turn to eat like everyone else." He turned away from me.

I didn't like the way he looked down his nose at me so I jerked on his coat tail again. I said, "Well, darlin', I am not interested in eating right now. I am interested in finding a restroom and you better be interested in me finding it, too. You have out here in your vestibule, a famous movie star who is dancing a jig in a pair of diamond-studded cowboy boots because she's about to wet on your floor. If you don't get her to a restroom before that happens, you are going to have a second Watergate scandal on your hands."

It was like parting the Red Sea. That man snapped his fingers and we were in the restroom. My only claim to fame is that I took Dale Evans to the restroom in the Watergate Apartments. The point of the story is this: Because I was able to communicate what the problem was in a way he was able to understand it, he was able to take care of it. Until you learn to communicate, you're going to have a problem getting to the top of the ladder.

No. 4. You're conduct both inside and outside the office is important.

YOUR REPUTATION is important to your successful climb up that ladder. Outside the office, on the streets of your city, you are the business you represent.

In Little Rock, Arkansas, when I'm out on the streets of the city, I am Arkansas Education Television. I am the Chamber of Commerce, the Salvation Army, and the Nazarene Church because these are organizations that I represent and they see these organizations through me. That's exactly the way it is with you. Whatever company you work for, you are their ambassador and you should act like it. The higher up the rung you are, the more important this fact is.

You say, "It's nobody's business what I do after hours." It's your company's business if you are really serious about wanting to climb that ladder. Keep your act clean.

No. 5. Be dependable.

LET YOUR WORD BE YOUR BOND. Be honest about what your product will do or won't do. About what your project will accomplish.

My dad was a used car salesman and you know what people say about used car salesmen. But my dad, at the age of 80, was still selling cars to the third and fourth generations of families because they had been told, "What Vick Gray says it is, it is." That's the kind of reputation you want to build.

I had tenants in my building that I had with me nearly 40 years. They moved in the first three months I was managing the building. They even moved from one building to another with me and when they were asked why, they would say, "Because Jane will do what she she tells me she will do. It doesn't have to be written in the clause of the lease. Her word is good enough." That's the kind of reputation you must build for yourself in any endeavor if you want to go to the top.

Be on time. Keep your appointments. Get out reports you promised. Answer those phone calls and return them.

Your company would rather have a second-best worker who is dependable than the best worker who is not. Be dependable.

No. 6. Be an active volunteer in your community.

VOLUNTEERING WILL OPEN MORE DOORS for you than a college education will because you will become well-known in your area. You will rub elbows with very important people in your community. Every fund-raiser in your city and every big community project is chaired by a "big dog." The presidents of the banks. The CEOs of the utilities. It may be in name only. They may not do the work but they chair it. If you volunteer for one of their causes, they will remember it and they will be able to help you open the doors. Besides, you get back more than you ever give to a volunteer effort. The personal perks of my life have not come from managing office space or buildings but the volunteer efforts I have put forth. I have traveled places and met famous people and received awards that this little girl from Little Rock would never have but for the volunteer efforts of my life.

President Bush once said, "Get interested in something and your life will sing." The volunteer efforts of my life are what have made my life "sing." Find yourself a good cause and go volunteer. It will pay off.

Jane was named Arkansas Woman of Style by RSVP in 1988.

No. 7. Be nice to the people you meet along life's way.

THE SALES CLERK. THE WAITRESS. The delivery boy. The clerical worker. You never know when these people will start climbing the ladder and they will remember you if you were nice to them.

When I worked at the employment agency, there was a delivery boy who brought our supplies every day. A nice high school kid. The others in the office would sign the ticket without even looking up. I took a liking to him. He impressed me as someone who was going to do something some day. I liked him. I started asking him to have coffee with me every day. When he would come in, we would have a coffee break and I would listen to him about his girlfriends and school and the courses he was going to take in college. After a few months, he got a better job and I didn't see him for years and years.

After he got out of college, I began to read about him in the business pages. Where he got a job. Where he moved up in a position. Some bigger company snatched him up. He just went right on up the ladder.

After I began to manage the 1515 Building and was trying to fill it, I read where he had been made vice-president of a large corporation in Little Rock, in charge of leasing. Can you believe it? I called and made an appointment. When his secretary announced me, he came running out into the waiting room. He hugged me. He kissed me on both cheeks. He patted me. He introduced me to his entire firm as the lady he had talked about who was so nice to him when he was just a delivery boy.

I told him why I was there. I had a building to fill. "I understand that you're in charge of leasing. Do you have any of your offices that you need to move somewhere?"

He not only moved a portion of his businesses into my building, he went out and scouted for me among other VIPs in the city. He helped me fill that building in three months. I wasn't nice to him when he was a delivery boy because I knew he was going to become someone important. I was nice to him because I was supposed to be. You are supposed to be nice to everyone you meet in life, no matter what their station. Also, be as nice to your small client as you are to your big client. When that small client starts growing, they will remember how nice you were to them when they were small.

No. 8. Attitude.

YOUR ATTITUDE DETERMINES if the other people in the office even want to have lunch with you. As you get older, your attitude will determine if your own grandkids will even want to come see you. Your attitude also determines your climb up the ladder.

You cannot be smart enough and you cannot work hard enough and you cannot know enough about your product to be successful with a negative attitude. You can run off as many people as the others in the business can bring in. There is nothing wonderful about a surly, nasty, argumentative, critical, negative attitude. If you have an attitude problem, you better start working on it.

My definition of a positive attitude is someone who enjoys the scenery, even when they are forced to take a detour.

This is a true story. The facts are true. It deals with senior citizens. Senior citizens don't have a corner on negative attitudes. Negative attitudes usually start when you are young because people decide whether they are going to be happy or miserable. They choose how they will live while young. The older they get, the worse it gets. But, there are lots of young negative people.

One of my volunteer efforts has been to help with Meals on Wheels. I used to go pick up meals at a church in Little Rock and carry them every Friday morning to a little neighborhood. I asked for the same neighborhood so I could get to know the people there. There were five people in this one neighborhood who received Meals on Wheels.

I always went to one house first because I knew I would leave there singing. I will be "up" and that's the way I want to face the rest of the day. This particular day, I picked up the five meals and went to this first home. I knocked on the door and waited on the lady to come to the door. She had bad arthritis, walked with a walker, and could barely open the door with her hands.

When she saw me, she said, "Oh, you sweet darling angel precious beautiful thing." Now, you know why I like to go see her! But that's the way she greeted everyone. She said, "You are so wonderful to bring me my meal! You're so precious to do this."

"Honey, let's go see what we've got."

She said, "It'll be good. It always is! I don't know what kind of good cooks they have at that church but everything they cook is wonderful."

"Let's see....there's fried chicken."

"Oh, that's wonderful," she said. "I just love fried chicken! They feed us chicken a lot but it's good for us. I've read that it's better for us than red meat. They cook it so good. It's always so tender. Whether they fry it, bake it, or broil it, it's always wonderful!"

I said, "You've got cream potatoes and gravy."

"Aren't they smart? They know us old folks don't have good teeth and it's hard to eat a lot of things. They know we can eat cream potatoes and gravy. Aren't they wonderful?!"

"Darling, you've also got cherry cobbler."

"Cherry is my favorite! How do they know that I have never had enough cherry cobbler in my life!"

I opened her milk for her and sat down and we talked about the kids and the Lord. Finally, I said, "I've got to go and get these meals to the other people."

I let myself out and took three other meals around and I always saved one house for the last. I knew I was going to leave there dragging. My spirits would be low when I walked out of that house.

I knocked on the door and a woman came running to the door. She didn't have arthritis like the other woman. She said, "Well, it's about time! You're just about to starve me to death!"

I said, "Honey, it's not even noon yet. Your meal is still warm."

She said, "I don't know what I'm fussing about. It won't be fit to eat when I get it. It never is. Those folks at that church can't cook nothing fit to eat."

"Today, you've got fried chicken."

"Awww. Chicken! That must be the cheapest old meat they can buy. They just feed it to us all the time. It's never fit to eat. I don't care if they fry it, bake it, or broil it, it's tough and chewy. I can't even eat the stuff!"

I said, "You've got cream potatoes and gravy and I know you can chew that."

"They'll be lumpy! They always are!"

"At least you've got homemade cobbler."

"It'll probably be cherry. I can't stand cherry!"

I threw it on the table and went out the front door. She came running after me and said, "Why don't you stay and talk to me. Nobody ever stays and talks to me!"

"Well, somebody else is going to have to. I have to go."

I got in the car and I put my head in my hands. I said, "Lord, you've got to help me with this one. Here it is, the same day, the same neighborhood, the same age people, the same menu. One lady, I could hardly break away from because she was such a joy. The other one, I couldn't slap her food fast enough on the table to get out of there. What is it?"

It's attitude. If you have an attitude problem, you better work on it or you will never make it to the top.

No. 9. Follow up.

WHEN WE GO AFTER A NEW CUSTOMER we just roll out the red carpet to get them. We take them out to lunch and we shower them with attention until we finally get their business. But too often we put them on the back burner while we go after a new prospect. We should treat that customer the same way we did to get him—or it won't be long until someone else will woo him away from us.

A man died and got to the pearly gates. St. Peter said, "Well, you qualify, so go on in." Up jumped the devil in front of the man and said, "I've been looking for the right person to go down to Hell for 24 hours and come back up and tell people that Hell is nothing like the preacher says it is."

The man said, "For sure, can I come back up in 24 hours?"

"Absolutely," said the devil.

"St. Peter said, "You better be careful, he's a liar."

The man said, "I've always wondered if Hell was what they say. I can take anything for 24 hours, so I'm gonna try it."

The devil lifted the lid and dropped him in. He could not believe it. Blue skies, white clouds, birds singing, flowers blooming, fish jumping. It was beautiful. Around the corner was the finest casino he had ever seen. Tunica has nothing as fine. All food and drinks were free. So were the chips. And a group of beautiful girls fawning all over him, getting him anything he wanted. At the end of 24 hours the devil took him back to St. Peter and said, "Well, how was it?"

"Hell is nothing like they say. It was wonderful."

The devil asked, "Are you ready to go back for Eternity?"

St. Peter said, "Remember, he said it was for Eternity."

"Well, I can do what I've been doing for Eternity. Let's go."

The devil lifted the lid, dropped him in and there was darkness, fire and brimstone, crying, yelling, and gnashing of teeth.

The man said, "This is not what you showed me yesterday."

"Yesterday, you were a prospect. Today, you're a customer."

No. 10. Be Serious.

YOU HAVE TO BE SERIOUS about your job if you really want to climb to the top of the ladder. You cannot be lack-luster about it or take a ho-hum attitude. You have to be serious.

The CIA put out notice that they were going to hire a new agent. After going through the many applications, they narrowed it down to three—two men and a woman. They notified them to come in for a final interview and to bring their spouse with them. They called the first man into a room, explained to him that a CIA agent had to be able to follow their orders for anything they were asked to do, no questions asked. Just do it. The man understood and really wanted the job. He was then given a pistol and told to go into the next room where his wife was and shoot her. He said, "Are you crazy? I'll not shoot my wife."

"That's very noble of you. I don't blame you. But we can't use you as you have to do exactly what we tell you to."

The man left in a huff.

The second man came in, was told the CIA expected him to do what they said, no questions asked, no hesitation. He said, "OK, I can do that and I really need the job."

They gave him the pistol and told him to go in the next room and shoot his wife. He started crying but said he would try. In a few minutes he came back out, still crying, and said, "I can't do it. She's the mother of my children and I love her. I can't do it."

"That's very noble of you. I don't blame you. But we can't use you."

Then they called in the woman and told her the same thing. She took the pistol, went into the room with her husband and eventually they heard five shots ring out. Then they heard the awfulest noise—screaming, yelling, banging, furniture hitting the wall. It sounded like they were tearing up the room. Then, everything got quiet. The woman came out, blood all over her, clothes half torn off, her hair down in her face. They said, "What in the world happened?"

She said, "Why, some fool put blanks in that gun and I had to kill him with a chair."

So, you have to be serious to get ahead.

No. 11. Enthusiasm.

YOU CAN SELL ANYTHING if you are enthusiastic enough about it. How do you expect anyone to buy your product, get excited about your project, or anything else you're trying to sell to them if you yourself aren't enthusiastic about it?

In the beginning, they may not be the least bit interested. But they will want to buy it to see if it's as wonderful as you think it is.

There was a little boy who's papa traveled every week. Left home on Monday. Came home on Friday. Every Friday, he brought him a toy or a gift of some kind. This particular Friday, he came in with a little live turtle. On the top of the turtle was printed the name "Tommy." That was the name of the little boy. The little boy was so thrilled with this gift. He had never had anything in his life that pleased him like this turtle did. If he went to bed, he took the turtle. If he went to the kitchen, he took the turtle. If he went to the bathroom, he took the turtle. The entire week he loved that turtle.

Papa came home the next Friday and the little boy ran to the car and fell on the ground in total hysterics.

"Son, what is the matter?"

"Oh, Papa, my turtle has died! He's dead! He's dead!"

"That's all right. We'll just get you another little turtle."

"I don't want another turtle! This one was named Tom after me and I don't want another turtle. He's dead!"

"Son, if you'll quit crying, I'm going to tell you what we're going to do. We're going to give that turtle the best funeral a turtle has ever had in this world!

"I want you to go get an empty shoe box. You take it to Mama and ask her for some of that red satin material from the new Valentine blouse she's sewing. You ask her to put it in the shoe box and that'll be it's little coffin.

"You know that prize rose bush in the back yard that we won't even let you walk around, let alone play around?"

"Yes, sir."

"You get a pair of scissors. You can cut three roses off that bush. Any three you want, big or little. We're going to lay those on top of that coffin.

"Then, I want you to go out in this neighborhood and gather any kid who can make a noise of any kind with an instrument. If they've got a bugle, a drum, a tambourine, or horn, or two sticks they can hit together. Anything to make noise. Bring them to the back yard. We're going to line them up, put that turtle on the red satin, lay those roses across it, and we're going to march up and down every street and alley in this neighborhood and have a funeral march that will be so wonderful that the TV cameras will come out and it will be on the 6 o'clock news."

The little boy did just what he said. He got the shoe box, the red satin, and cut the roses. He went out and got the kids and they were in the backyard lined up in a row, marching to time, beating their little drums, blowing their horns, getting ready for that march. Papa went in to get the turtle. He came out and he said, "Son, do I have good news for you!"

"What's that, Papa?"

"Honey, your turtle wasn't dead. It was just sunning in the window."

"Kill it, Daddy, kill it!!!"

You see, you can sell anything if you are enthusiastic.

No. 12. Give credit where credit is due.

BECAUSE IF IT WERE NOT FOR GOD who has given you and blessed you with a sound body and a sound mind, you wouldn't even be able to climb that ladder of success. And, also thank Him for the hot water vats of your life. Because without them, you wouldn't be as strong as you are today. Remember, it was Joseph who said, "What the devil meant for harm, God used for good." And that's exactly what God can do with the hot water vats of your life if you'll just trust Him and allow Him. Be sure you give Him proper credit and then go get 'em!

CHAPTER 6

Sharing

Jane

COLOSSIANS 3:17

Sharing

Turning it over to God

EVERYONE CAN TELL ABOUT AN EMBARRASSING THING that happened in their life. We could all have a good laugh. I've had many funny, embarrassing situations happen in my life and I could fill a book with those stories!

For example, I managed an office building for forty years and I showed men the office space they could rent. One day, I was getting ready to show a couple of men some office space and I went to the restroom first. I had on one of those big tulip-shaped skirts that flare out all around the ankles. I came out of the restroom and had accidently tucked my skirt into my panty hose. I was walking down the hall and the two men were behind me and one of them finally said, "Mrs. Krutz, you better see about your dress." It was embarrassing, but I laughed about it.

Camel Dowry

THERE WAS ALSO THE TIME I was on a tour of Israel. I was in a store in the city of Jerusalem. There was an Arab merchant I was trying to purchase something from and I made the mistake of calling him "Sugar." I call people that all the time. Ted told me I call everyone "Sugar" and "Darling" because I can't remember anybody's name.

I said "Sugar" to the merchant and he grabbed me by both arms and started screaming at me at the top of his voice in his native tongue. I didn't know what he was saying. He was shaking me and screaming at me. I thought, "Oh, dear Jesus, help me. I've done something wrong or committed a sin."

I began to tell the interpreter to tell the merchant that I was sorry if I made him mad and to please, please forgive me. She laughed. "You didn't make him mad. He's yelling to see who owns you. He wants to pay twenty camels and buy you."

I was so elated. "Oh, let me get to a telephone—we'll call Ted Krutz back in Arkansas and tell him there is a man somewhere who is willing to pay twenty camels to get me."

The interpreter said, "Honey, I wouldn't brag too much. He said he would pay sixty camels, but he knew you were too old to bear children." True story.

The Picnic

THERE ARE MOMENTS IN OUR LIFE when we can laugh. But have you ever had an experience that was so embarrassing that you could not find humor in it? It's called humiliation.

Several years ago, I had an embarrassing situation that was so humiliating that to this day, I find no humor in it. I am not yet able to laugh about it but I'm going to tell you about it because it dovetails into what I want to share with you concerning sharing in the joy of Jesus.

My daughter Vikki, her husband Pat, and their three children had lived in Poplar Bluff, Missouri for about twelve years. He changed jobs and moved to Conway. I was thrilled to death because they were moving within thirty minutes of where I lived. I was excited as I could be.

They moved into a rented house and had not even unpacked much when a neighbor invited them to a special musical at a large church in Conway. They didn't attend there but she invited them to the musical and they went.

Vikki said the women were so friendly to her. She had never been treated so well and they insisted that the next week she come to a women's fellowship at one of their homes. It was going to be a picnic and a pool party and she could invite a guest to come with her since she was new and didn't know anyone. She said, "I would love to bring my mother and my sister."

"That will be great. We would love to have them."

Vikki called me and said, "Mama, you and Janie have to come go with me. This picnic and pool party is going to be in a gated community in Conway where I hear there isn't a home there less than a quarter of a million dollars. I would be intimidated to go by myself. You've got to go."

I love to go anywhere and I was thrilled just to be with Vikki. Janie and I agreed to go. Vikki told us that every person was to bring a picnic lunch and she would fix all three of our lunches. She said, "All you have to do is show up about 10:30. It starts at 11:00."

Janie drove down from Heber Springs. I drove from Little Rock. We went in our cute new little summer dresses and we arrived at Vikki's house at 10:30, ready to go.

When she met us at the door, she was still in her robe. She was frantic. Her hair was wet from sweat. The air conditioning had gone out that morning and the plumbing had backed up in her bathroom. The landlord was out of town and she had spent the entire morning trying to find a plumber and a serviceman to help her. The temperature was 100 degrees. She was dripping wet and there was still no air on in the house. The plumber had been there and repaired the bathroom so she took a shower real quick and got dressed.

I said, "Darling, do you have our lunches ready?"

"Mother, that's something else. I was going to the store to buy something nice to take. I guess I have something I can throw together. I'm glad it's just a picnic where we can take our own lunch."

So she looked into the kitchen cabinet and found a loaf of bread with six slices in it and two of them were heels. That was enough for three sandwiches. She had peanut butter and jelly. I was all right with that. "I haven't had peanut butter and jelly in a long time. I like it and that will be fine."

She put the sandwiches together and two of them had a heel on them. She had a big bag of potato chips that were down to the very bottom—you know how the chips crumble in the bottom. She got three little baggies and divided those crumbs into those little baggies.

She said, "Thank goodness I have some Little Debbie cakes. At least we can have a dessert."

Vikki put the sandwiches, the little baggies of potato chips, and a Little Debbie in sacks. We each got a little paper sack. We rolled them up and went to the party.

It was a gated community where security had to call and get clearance for us to get in. When we drove up to that house, it covered more than half a city block. It was the most gorgeous home

I think I have ever seen or been inside. There is nothing in Chenault Valley, Little Rock bigger or prettier than that home.

We rang the doorbell and the hostess came to the door. She was so gracious and said, "Oh, Vikki, we've been waiting on you. We're so glad to have you."

"This is my sister Janie and this is my mother."

"You mean your mother is Miss Jane on Channel 2?"

"Yes."

"I'm so thrilled and the other women will be so thrilled! I had no idea your mother was Miss Jane. We've watched her for years. Let me have your lunches."

We were holding them and hiding them behind our purses. She said, "I have to have them so I can number them."

I said, "Oh, no, honey. Vikki had a problem at home this morning and she didn't have time to go to the grocery store. We just have a little lunch and we would prefer to keep them ourselves."

She literally tore them from our hands. "Oh, no. This is the fun part. We number them and draw names and then everybody eats the lunch that they get. Besides, we give prizes to the prettiest boxes that they are brought in."

If I had it to do over, that's where I would have turned and left. I would have turned around and said, "I'm sorry. We misunderstood what this was. We'll come next year—you can invite us then."

But I was already in shock and did not have enough sense to turn around and leave. She took us to the backyard. It was as big as the house. There was a kidney-shaped swimming pool with orchids floating in the water. A gazebo with a lace-covered table was covered with the lunches the other ladies had brought. When she escorted us to the backyard she said, "You are not going to believe it, girls, but

Vikki's mother is Miss Jane from Channel 2." This, of course, made it even harder for us.

I got a look at the table in the gazebo and what was on top of it. The first thing I saw was a big round hat box that had been covered in floral chintz with a big satin bow on top. The next box was a pink satin-covered box with long stemmed pink roses tied into the bow. Every box there was equal to this.

The one that really caught my eye was a wooden birdcage—a beautifully decorated birdcage. It had a bunch of sugar-covered grapes cascading off the top. Inside, you could see a lace doily with a chicken salad croissant, fruit salad, and homemade lemon meringue pie.

We, again, tried to explain why we didn't want our lunches added to the collection but she absolutely said, "No, honey, that's perfectly all right." She put numbers on our sacks and added them to the table.

From that moment, until I stood up to leave, not one of the three of us spoke another word. Both of my daughters talk as much as I do and Janie talks louder. We did not speak another word. We nodded or shook our heads but we did not speak.

They finally got around to drawing numbers. Janie got the birdcage. Vikki got the satin box with the roses on top. I got the box with the chintz and satin ribbon. Those also happened to be the first, second, and third prizes for the most beautiful boxes there. You not only got to eat the lunch but take the boxes home with you.

The three ladies who got our sacks happened to sit close to us. Those three women were Spirit-filled, I have no doubt. They never made a face. The didn't roll their eyes. They didn't make a snide remark. They were as gracious as they could be. They opened up those little paper sacks and took out those peanut butter and jelly sandwiches with the heel on them. One of them said, "Oh, I haven't had peanut butter in years. How quaint!"

Another one said, "I just love Little Debbie cakes!"

We sat there munching on sugar-covered grapes while they were licking their fingers as they reached into the plastic bags for those potato chips because they were hungry.

This is not a preacher story that is made up to make a point. Every detail is the truth and that's why, to this day, I don't find it funny.

The second we got through eating, I stood and said something for the first time, "I have an appointment and need to leave at once."

We left our boxes on the table and did not take them with us. We ran out of that house.

Vikki never went back to church there. To this day, when I think about it, I want to cry because it really was that humiliating. I am sure, to this day, when any one of those women see me on AETN, they repeat this story to whoever is watching it with them.

Bob Benson

I WANT TO SHARE A STORY BY BOB BENSON. If you did not have the privilege of knowing Bob Benson before he died, look him up in Heaven. He's worth knowing.

Bob Benson wrote a story and gave a message entitled "A Bologna Sandwich." He tells about being invited to a Sunday school picnic on a Saturday afternoon at the park. Each person was to bring their own lunch and the church would furnish the iced tea. He had worked late and had not had time to go shopping. The only thing he could find in the ice box was a dried up piece of bologna and two pieces of stale bread. There was just enough mustard in the jar that he got it all over his knuckles when he tried to get it out. That's what he fixed and he put it in a little brown sack and carried it to the picnic. Bob sat at the end of the table and spread out his bologna sandwich. The folks next to him had brought a feast. The lady was a good cook and had worked all day preparing the picnic lunch. Fried chicken. Baked beans. Potato salad. Homemade rolls. Sliced tomatoes. Pickles. Olives. Celery. Two big homemade chocolate pies. They spread it out next to him and he said, "I sat there with my bologna sandwich."

Then, they said, "Why don't we just put it all together and share with one another?"

"Oh, no. I couldn't do that."

"Come on. We've got plenty of chicken and pie and everything. And, we just love bologna sandwiches. Why don't we just put it all together?"

So they did. He said, "I sat there eating like a king—when I came like a pauper. One day, it dawned on me that God had been saying just that sort of thing to me. Why don't you take what you have and what you are, and I'll take what I have and what I am and we'll share it together.

"I began to see that when I put what I had, was, am, and hope to be with what He is, I had stumbled upon the bargain of a lifetime."

I think of myself sometimes sharing with God. I think of how little I bring and how much He brings and invites me to share. I know I should be shouting from the house tops. I know I don't have enough love, faith, grace, mercy, or wisdom, but He does. He has all of these things in abundance and He said, "Let's just put it all together."

Consecration. Denial. Sacrifice. Commitment. Crosses. These were all hard words to me until I saw them in the light of sharing. It isn't just a case of me kicking in what I have because God is the biggest kid in the neighborhood and He wants everything all to Himself. He is saying,

"Everything I possess is available to you. Everything that I am and can be to a person, I will be to you.

When I think about it like that, it really amuses me to see someone running along through life hanging on to that little bag with a stale bologna sandwich in it saying, "God's not going to get my sandwich. No siree. This is mine. I made it all by myself."

It's not that God needs your sandwich. The fact is, you need His chicken. Go ahead and eat your old bologna sandwich as long as you can. When you can't stand its tastelessness or drabness any longer... when you get tired of running your own life by yourself and doing it your way...when you get tired of figuring out all the answers with no one to help...when you try to accumulate, and hold, grasp, and keep everything together in your own strength...when it gets to be too big of a load...when you begin to realize that, by yourself, you're never going to be able to fulfill your dream...I hope you'll remember that it does not have to be that way. You have been invited to something better. You have been invited to share in the very Being of God.

I want you to share with me in an exercise. Go to your kitchen and get a paper bag. Open it up and label it "God's Bag." Mentally and spiritually put into God's Bag every problem you have. Are you heartbroken? Is there something in your life that has absolutely broken your heart? Maybe you are not responsible for it at all. Maybe it's the loss of a loved one or a child or spouse and you just can't get on top of it. Put that heartache in the bag.

Do you have some habit you're trying to break? You've tried and tried, and it's still got the best of you. You know you can't really be a victorious Christian and keep that habit. Put it in the bag. Say, "God, I'm giving this habit to You and I'm going to trust You to help me get over it."

Is there some unresolved sin in your life? Is there something you haven't asked God to forgive you for that you're still slipping around and doing? Maybe no one else in the world knows about it—but God does. Put that sin in the bag and give that sin to God. Is it your attitude? Are you negative about every thing? If you are, put your attitude in this bag and say, "God, I'm going to let You help me have a more positive attitude because I'm not a witness for You when I'm negative about everything."

Do you have anger? Are you angry and mad about something that has happened to you? You may not really want to give up that anger. You may really want some revenge for it. God says, "Vengeance is Mine." Anger will eat you up, so put your anger in the bag.

Are you unforgiving toward someone? Has someone hurt you and done something ugly toward you? Maybe the person who has hurt you is even someone in the church. Or your husband. Child. Sister. Brother. Your parents or someone from your childhood. Have you ever really forgiven them? If you haven't, put that unforgiveness in the bag and say, "God, I'm going to forgive." The Bible is very plain that unless you forgive, He cannot forgive you. Unforgiveness will eat up the vessel that it is in. It's like acid. It will eat you up a long time before it harms the person you aren't forgiving. Put that unforgiveness and bitterness in the bag.

Are you worried about something? Are you worried about your health? Your children's health? Your job? Security? Something you're losing sleep over? Put it in the bag and say, "God, I'm going to let You lose sleep over this tonight and I'm going to sleep with the knowledge that You're going to take care of whatever problem I have.

Then, you may have to put yourself in the bag. Sometimes the hardest person to forgive is yourself. God will forgive you for a sin, but often you just keep hammering yourself in the head about it. That's the devil, because God has already forgotten about it. I love the song Gary Haines sings, "What Sin Are You Talking About?" God says, "I don't remember that anymore." Put your own forgiveness for yourself in the bag and give that to God.

The last thing is to put the unknown future—whatever is out there, whatever comes in the future...your health, your children, your family—put that in the bag. Think hard about it and whatever the Holy Spirit brings to your mind, put it in the bag.

Close up your bag and lay it on the altar. Then when the devil bring these things up to you, say, "You'll have to talk to God about that, old Devil—it's in *His* bag!

CHAPTER 7

Jane and Willie Oates

PROVERBS 8:14

ETN

Volunteering for educational television

IN 1963, AFTER THREE YEARS at KARK-TV, I was hired to manage the 1515 Building on West 7th Street directly across from the State Capitol. It changed my life. After working as a secretary behind the desk eight hours a day, I was free to go and come as I pleased as long as I kept the building full of tenants and the rent collected. It also allowed me to get to know all the politicians from the Governor on down, as they would come over from the capitol to eat in our restaurant. I had coffee every morning with the Supreme Court Justices and, sworn to secrecy, I listened to them discuss their cases for the day.

I also was able to volunteer for several good organizations. My bosses Claude Carpenter and Kay Matthews were smart enough to know that when I was out in the community volunteering, I was also advertising their building. It was during this time I got involved with the Chamber of Commerce and set records in selling local memberships. They later named their membership award The Jane Krutz Cup.

I loved every minute of the forty years I was a building manager. Twenty years at the 1515 building and twenty at the Executive Building, where I also had a wonderful boss, Donna VanEekeren. She also allowed me to do lots of volunteer work. I retired at the age of 75.

The real turning point in my life came when Senator Lee Reaves walked into the 1515 Building and asked for office space. It was 1964 and Rep. Willie Oates introduced a bill to start an education TV station in Arkansas. Senator Reaves was selected to direct the station. My first grandchild, Kyle, had just been born when I learned what educational television was all about. I said, "He's got to have this. What can I do to help?"

Senator Reaves suggested I start a Friends Volunteer Group, which I did one year before going on the air. When the building in Conway was finished, they allowed me to pull the switch to turn on the power. It has been a love affair ever since. Keeping good clean family-friendly programs on the air is our goal. The thrill of watching that one station in Conway grow into a state-wide network that reaches into every corner of the state has been wonderful. I'm so proud to have been a little part of it.

We did not start on our fundraising for ten years. For the first fundraiser, we were on the air for 72 straight hours. Fred Schmutz, the program director, and I were on camera almost that entire 72 hours. The whites of our eyes turned gray. After that, we went to the format we use now, a few hours each night for two weeks. In the beginning, I was on 16 nights straight. Now I'm on three to six nights during the pledge drives. Because of my volunteer service to the station, they named the studio The Jane Krutz Studio in 2007.

In 1995 PBS sent me to Washington to testify before a Congressional committee regarding funding cuts. After my ten minute speech, they said I was the only person who ever got a standing ovation from a Congressional committee. We also kept our funding.

AETN is still one of my top priorities, since I now have six great-grandchildren. I've received back so much more than I've ever given.

Jane Krutz testifies before the House Appropriations Committee

MR. CHAIRMAN, members of this subcommittee, I am Jane Krutz from Little Rock, a business woman and a volunteer. I was one of the founding members of the Friends Board for the Arkansas Education Network and I still serve on that Board.

We're a State Network of five public television stations serving the entire State of Arkansas. However, I'm here today to speak on behalf of America's public television stations representing 202 local licensees reaching 99% of American television households. It's a system that is free, it is in place and working now, and I am here to represent the public that depends on this system. In 1964, when I first heard about the concept of educational television, I was convinced that it was a learning opportunity that my children could not miss and so I am a volunteer. Now, after more than 30 years as an active volunteer, I am more convinced today than I was then that we must continue this necessary tool of education for my grandchildren and for yours. We're not in as safe a world as we were 30 years ago and we more than ever need it. I am here to tell you that the money that this Committee appropriated for public TV for this year, 1995, is one of the best bargains that you get for the Federal dollar and I'd like to tell you what the local television stations do with this financial support and how they serve the people. Services that help children learn, help adults learn to read and help high school dropouts get their GED diploma. Services that train day care providers and enable 1.8 million teachers to use quality instructional programming that reaches 29 million students, and the service that brings joy to the senior citizens and shut-ins. I would point out that when educational television was brought into outlying rural areas of America, many people were given their first glimpse of a New York ballet or an Italian opera. Now I don't know about ya'll but honey, where I came from, we couldn't even spell Pavarotti before PBS brought him to us and if you pull PTV away from them now, the next generation won't be able to spell it either (You notice he's not calling my hand on that don't you?). Well, some of you say that now cable has some of this type of programming. I must point out that 40% of the American families do not get cable. For some, it is not available, but most of them cannot afford it. So what good is A&E and Discovery and Disney? If we pull ETV, these families will be cut off from any cultural or educational programs and these are the families that need it the most. I would point out that public television stations work directly with local schools. They average five and a half hours a day programming for class room use. They broadcast overnight so that teachers can record and build a library of programs. Many of our rural schools could not afford the caliber of teachers and the resources for students that PTV brings into their classroom and these are the children who need it most. I would point out that commercial television has cut back children's educational programs to two hours a week. We program educational programs for children seven hours a day. Teachers have said that children entering kindergarten raised with Sesame Street, Mr. Rogers and like programs on ETV are one year ahead of the children who were not. Do we really want to push education for children back a year? I would point out that today over 4,000 adults are enrolled in the GED program in my state alone. And that in America, there are one and a half million productive adults who have obtained their high school diploma through the GED program for ETV. This program alone is worth funding public television. And they say that PTV is only for the rich and elite. I would point out that local PTV stations enable 325,000 tuition-paying students a chance to earn a college degree through television. I would point out that in this day when we're all concerned with violence, especially among our youth, ETV has no violence, period. If we pull funding then our kids are going to be left with the violence on all the other channels. You say, well now Jane, some of your programs have been real objectionable. Yes, a few have been and nobody screams louder or jumps higher than I do about them. And what you're looking at here is a Southern, fundamentalist far-right conservative. And we have run a few programs that I don't like. But we run so many more wonderful programs that everybody likes. Please don't throw out the baby with the bath water. During 1994 in Arkansas there were no less than 10 hours a day of objectionable programs on other networks. Now, I want you to know that I was married with children before I knew that the word "kinky" meant anything in the world besides an over-processed permanent. And do you know where I learned it? On daytime, prime time, network TV and it was not PBS. Now if we pull PTV our kids are going to have a heavy, steady dose of those kinds of programs and they don't invite viewers to call in with opinions. But I want you to know that we do. And we listen to those opinions, both pro and con, and we should listen because we're public TV. Remember this, our kids are going to watch TV and we can teach them with PTV a lot more than we can with anything else. How critical are those Federal dollars for the public television system? Well, it varies widely. Anywhere from 6% all the way to 54%. But the more important question is how critical are these Federal dollars for the public television system? The answer is, very critical. It's estimated that many small, rural stations will fold during the first year, and there goes our reach to 99% of the American PBS households. Without these stations in the system, programming is more expensive for the survivors. Then many more stations could close down the second year. Now some will survive, but certainly not be the public television as we know it today. Now some have said that public broadcasting should be privatized, whatever that means. If privatizing means seeking market-place sources of funds, we know what that means. We have a model. It's called commercial broadcasting. And we would lose what is different about public television. Do ya'll have any idea how important public television is to the public? Before I left Little Rock to come up here, I visited with many folks on this issue. They could not believe that you all are even considering doing away with or cutting their favorite programs. Now I'm not really sure that ya'll understand how serious this is going to be back home if you cut the public's television. Please consider this, that of the three public educational institutions in America, public schools, public libraries, and public television, more people can be touched by public television at any given moment than by the other two put together. And as a concerned parent and grandparent and citizen of this country, I'm here to ask you today to not rescind or cut the funding for public television, it is just so important. Thank you.

Jane's speech can be viewed at
www.c-spanvideo.org/program/PublicBroad

Jane speaks to the Arkansas audience on AETN during a fund raiser.

Jane dances a polka with Bobby Burgess from the Lawrence Welk Show in 1995.

Being Recognized

SINCE I HAVE APPEARED several times a year on AETN fund drives, starting in 1976, I am often recognized when I'm out and around town. Also, because AETN covers the entire state, I'm recognized in almost every area of the state.

Often, they do not recognize my face but the minute I speak, they know me. I was not aware I have such a distinctive voice but

Jane with youngest granddaughter
Sarah Jane Lay

Fred Schmutz and Jane
during a pledge drive.

Senator Lee Reaves (Director of AETN), Jane,
and Fred Schmutz (Program Director at AETN)

*Jane interviews
Muppets Bert and Ernie.*

Jane with Bill Valentine

Senator David Pryor, U.S. Congressman Ed Bethune, Jane, Governor Orval Faubus

apparently, I do. My daughter says, "Mother, don't ever try to rob a bank. They'll know you as soon as you say, "stick-em up.""

People are often shy about speaking to me and asking me if I'm "Miss Jane" on AETN. I always answer them warmly and thank them for watching the network. I answer any of their questions and listen to all their comments about the programs. The most repeated comment is, "My mother just loves you." I can't tell you how many times I've heard that. My husband used to get such a kick out of the different people who would recognize me. His favorite story, and he told it often, was about the elderly couple sitting in a Wendy's in Texarkana, Texas. When we walked in, they started pointing at me and talking to each other. When we walked past them to leave, the man said to his wife, "Well, thar she goes!"

I've had to learn to be careful in public, because just as sure as I get a little testy with a sales clerk or waiter, they will say, "Aren't you that lady on ETV?" Then, I have to apologize for being short with them but I bet they tell all their friends what a witch I really am. So I try to keep my act clean.

One day I ran to the grocery store in an old pair of blue jeans with my hair under a scarf. No makeup on. I made the mistake of talking to the checkout clerk. The woman behind me said, "Oh, you're Miss Jane on AETN." I crossed my fingers and said, "No." She said, "You sound exactly like her." I said, "Honey, my own children think I sound like her." And I hurried out as fast as I could.

ONE OF MY MOST EMBARRASSING moments was when Ted and I went on a vacation to celebrate my 60th birthday—remember that, my 60th. I had just lost mother and needed to get away. I was at my heaviest weight and bought an extra large knit suit to travel in—with an elastic waistband and a hangout shirt. The only pattern it came in was white and huge black polka dots all over it. Ted said I looked like Howdy Doody in it. But it was comfortable and I wasn't going to see anyone I knew on the beach in Florida. I had sprained my foot the day before we left and it hurt so bad I didn't sleep all that night. When I got ready to leave the next morning, I put on no makeup and just brushed through my hair. About a block from the house, Ted got a look at me and said, "Can't you do something to yourself? You look terrible." I said, "No, I'm hurting too bad to care. I'm going to sleep. Wake me for lunch."

At noon, he woke me in Vicksburg, Mississippi at a Shoney's. My foot was still hurting so bad that I sat down at the first booth and told him to fix my plate. Two ladies sat at the next table. One was about my age, the other was very old and bent over. I soon realized it was mother and daughter. The daughter was so helpful to her mother and talked so sweetly to her. It made me so lonesome for my mother. I leaned over and said, "Your daughter is so sweet to you." She yelled, "Huh?" I repeated a little louder. Again, she yelled, "Huh?" This time I yelled it real loud. She yelled, "Yes, she treats me this way all the time." Again, speaking very loud, "How old are you?" She yelled, "87!" When I realized everyone in the room had stopped eating and was looking at us. I tried to turn the volume of my voice down a little, but still loud enough for her to hear. I said, "My mother was 83." She yelled, "83!" I said, 'Yes." "Well, you don't look a day over 70, not 83." Ted was about to fall on the floor laughing. I walked out of the restaurant as fast as I could with my sore foot.

Two ladies came running out after me and when they caught up, they started hugging and kissing me. They said, "Oh, Miss Jane, our mother just loves you." (See, there it is again). And we can't wait to tell her we got to meet you."

Rev. Phil Hathcock, President of the AETN Foundation presents Jane the plaque naming the AETN Studio the "Jane Krutz Studio."

"Now, I know you don't get AETN in Vicksburg."

They said, "No, we're from Pine Bluff. Just passing through. We didn't recognize you when we saw you but the minute you talked, we knew it was you." I started apologizing for looking so bad. I told them about my bad foot, no makeup, had not fixed my hair and so forth. One woman said, "Well, I have to admit, you look better on TV than you do in person."

I HAVE SEVERAL GIRL FRIENDS who have been friends most of my life, some since childhood. We get together often for lunch, trying out new restaurants in town. We started out with about 10, now we're down to five. Of course we are all in our 80s now, so what can you expect?

In 2004, Little Rock put in new street car tracks in downtown, taking the street cars across the Arkansas River Bridge into North Little Rock. It has become a tourist attraction and is a nice ride around the downtown areas of both cities.

We gals decided we would go on the streetcar ride after lunch. We had eaten at a restaurant on Main Street in North Little Rock where the street car ran. Afterwards, we went out and sat on a bench waiting for it to come pick us up. We asked a man passing by what time the streetcar would arrive. He told us it did not stop at that corner and we would have to walk about three blocks up the street to get on. I told him we could not walk that far as all of us were on walking canes and having a hard time walking. He said, "They will not stop at this corner."

"You wanna bet?"

We watched until we saw the streetcar coming toward us. When it was a block away, I stepped out into the middle of the tracks and started waving my cane over my head. The conductor put on his brakes and stopped a few feet short from me. He got out and said, "Lady, what are you doing?"

I explained that we five ladies, all with canes, could not walk to the regular stop and wanted to ride the car. He said, "But I don't stop at this corner."

I said, "Well you have now, so just let us get on."

After a dirty look and some huffing he finally agreed. I got on first. The step was real high and I had to use both hands on the hand rails to pull myself up. I threw my purse, coat, and cane on the street car floor and pulled myself onto the car. As I was leaning down to pick them up, two men jumped out of their seats and literally stepped over me and jumped off the street car. I thought, "How rude! They could have at least waited until I had picked up my stuff to get off. How rude!"

When I looked around, I saw why they had gotten off so fast. There on the street lay poor Syble. Her feet were on the high step and her head was on the curb. She had fallen backwards when she tried to get on. Luckily, when the men picked her up, the only thing really hurt was her pride. Since the price was only 25¢ for seniors, I paid for all five of us.

Fompy followed Syble, then Helen, and Mary was last. Mary had a broken foot, walked very slowly, and was also hard of hearing. She did not hear me say I had already paid for her and she started digging in her purse for money. I kept saying, "Mary, I've already paid." Each time I said it louder until I was yelling at her. She finally understood and started looking for a seat.

We were all seated, except for Mary, and the only empty seats were by strangers. Mary walked—very slowly—to the back of the car looking for a seat. She returned—very slowly—to the front of the car. I kept saying, "Mary, sit down." Each time, I said it louder until I was yelling. She went to the back of the car and then to the front of the car three times—very slowly.

The conductor said, "I can't start the car until that lady sits down." On her third trip up the aisle, I stood up and pushed her down into a seat yelling at the top of my voice, "Mary, sit down!" By this time everyone on the car was laughing out loud. I thought, "Thank you, Lord, all these folks are tourists. Nobody knows who we are. "

About that time, I heard from the back of the car, "Why, that's Miss Jane on Channel 2." Oh well, laughter is good for the soul.

BUT THE STORY THAT TAKES THE CAKE was when we were traveling from Florida and were on a long stretch of highway that had no service stations or restaurants, and therefore, no restrooms. I was doing a jig in the front seat, begging Ted to hurry and get me to a rest room. We finally saw the big red "M" in the distance. When Ted pulled up and stopped, I jumped out and ran, not even shutting the car door. I ran back to the women's room (they are always at the back), praying the whole way that a stall would be empty. The first stall was the big handicapped one and I ran and sat down without bothering to close the stall door. Since the door opened out into the large center room, I could not reach it to close it.

About that time, another woman came into the restroom. Remember, I am still sitting and I say, "Honey would you mind closing the door. I can't get to it." She said, "I'll be glad to." Then, she made eye contact with me and exclaimed, "You're Miss Jane on AETN!" She then walked into the stall, closed the door behind her and locked it. I knew she was not aware of what she had done. We were knees to knees. She's standing and I'm sitting. She first tells me how her mother loves me (see, there it is again). Then, she goes through all the programs she loves and the ones she's not crazy about, and wants to know why we took certain programs off. Folks think I control the program schedule, which I don't. But I try to answer all the questions and thank them for watching. I finally said, "Honey, you'll have to go out for me to get up." She then realized what she had done. She said, "Oh, no, I'm so sorry."

As she went out, she said, "I can't wait to tell Mother I met Miss Jane."

"Well, please don't tell her where."

It's been a joy meeting all the people through the years and listening to their stories. The fans have been so faithful to help, by pledging during the fund drives, and faithful to pay their pledges. God bless them every one and may they enjoy their coffee mugs.

*Allen Weatherly, AETN executive director, and Jane
receive a check from the UAMS College of Nursing.*

CHAPTER 8

Mistaken Identities

Mistaken Identities

I just beg for money on television.

I SERVED ON THE National Friends Board of Educational Television and attended all of the national conferences. One year, we met in Washington, D.C. All of the ladies serving on the Friends Board sat together at meal time. From the first day, the maître d', a middle-aged man, paid a lot of extra attention to me at every meal. He would meet me at the door as I came in, pull my chair out for me, fix my napkin in my lap, and was at my beck and call. He was nice to the other ladies but did not show them the extra attention he showed me. If my glass was half-empty, he immediately filled it. He almost hovered over me until the ladies began teasing me that he was struck on me and they were going to tell Ted that I had a boyfriend. I even laughed about it because he did seem extremely attentive to me. This went on the entire week. On the last day, at breakfast, when he pulled out my chair for me to sit down, he said, "You will never know, Governor Richards, what a thrill it has been for me to wait on you this week."

I am sorry that I did not just say "thank you" and let him think that he had waited on Governor Ann Richards of Texas. He turned red, turned away, and I never saw him again.

THE SUMMER OF 2001, my family was in Branson, Missouri. We spent the day at Silver Dollar City. It was an extremely hot day and my daughter, Janie, had a fainting spell. An ambulance was called and I got in with her to go to the hospital in downtown Branson. We went into the emergency room and it was packed. I told Janie we would probably be there all day. But within ten minutes a nurse came out and took Janie and me into an examination room. We were surprised at getting in so soon. After getting information from Janie, they turned to me and said, "Who are you?" I said, "I'm Mama." They said, "We thought so." Every few minutes, more nurses and interns would come and visit with Janie and then turned to me and say, "So you're Mama." This went on for about thirty minutes, with more groups of nurses and interns coming and going. Finally, an intern walked in with a pencil and piece of paper.

He said, "I have been designated to get your autograph to go onto our celebrity board."

I said, "Look here. I know you don't get AETN in Branson, Missouri.

They said, "AETN?"

"Yes, I'm Miss Jane on AETN." Thinking that was how they recognized me.

"Oh, no. We thought you were Raymond's mother on "Everybody Loves Raymond."

I wish I had had enough sense to sign the autograph "Doris Roberts, Raymond's Mama."

I WAS IN A GIFT SHOP in Heber Springs, Arkansas when a lady came up to me and said, "Are you the lady on TV?"

I said, "Yes."

"Are you on AETN?"

"Yes."

"Oh, can I hug you? Can I kiss you?"

"Yes."

"I have every one of your cookbooks."

"Oh, no, Honey. I'm not Phyllis who cooks. I'm Miss Jane who begs for money."

She turned and walked away without another word.

Jane Krutz
Commissioner
501.663.5437

www.aetn.org

Be more PBS

Arkansas Educational Television Network
350 S. Donaghey • Conway, AR 72034

CHAPTER 9

Serving

Billy Graham and Jane at the luncheon before the Billy Graham Crusade.

MATTHEW 28:18

The Billy Graham Crusade

Busy busy busy

ONE OF THE MOST REWARDING THINGS I've ever done was serving for one year on the Billy Graham Executive Committee before the crusade in Little Rock in 1989. I was chosen as the Lay representative for the Church of the Nazarene. Every denomination was represented by a lay person. Buddy Sutton was the General Chairman and there were chairmen chosen for things like transportation, housing, hospitality, and so forth.

Several local pastors served on the committee. We all met once a week for a prayer meeting and then went into a business session... about thirty total. During the last month, we met every morning.

Some friends said, "Jane, you may be disappointed if you get to know the inside working of the organization. That has happened to some other religious leaders."

I was not afraid of that and sure enough, after a year, I had even more respect for the Billy Graham work than ever before. Because I saw how above-board and straight on it was. Since my office was just a few blocks from their headquarters, I was chosen as a co-signer of their checks. I saw where all the money went and they did not spend one dime on anything unnecessary.

I had mentioned that we should keep snacks in the work room for staff and volunteers. They said, "Oh, we can't spend money on things like that." I called my high school friend, J. B. Bond, who owned Tender Pop popcorn company and told him we needed him to furnish us with a popcorn machine and popcorn for the office. He asked for how long.

"One year."

"Oh, Jane. I can't do that."

"It won't hurt you to make a few points with the Lord. You make enough off your theaters' popcorn and nachos to pay for that."

The next day, he delivered the machine and kept us in fresh popcorn for the entire year.

Another thing I was impressed by was the fact that the transportation chairman had made arrangements for a limo service to furnish transportation each night for Billy Graham and his entire group. But we were told "Mr. Graham will not ride in a limo."

"But they are furnishing it for free."

"People might think they are paying for it with their offering. Please furnish just medium-size cars—not even a Cadillac or Lincoln. We must be careful of perception." They were transported in Fords and Pontiacs.

I remember my cousin, Eloise Knippers, telling about Ruth Graham turning down the offer of a full-length mink coat from a wealthy admirer. The lady said, "I have a closet full of fur coats and I want to share this with you."

Ruth Graham said, "I love fur coats and would enjoy wearing one, but people would think we had used their offering to pay for it. Please share it with someone who does not have a coat." These are some of the reasons the Billy Graham ministry has been so successful.

The Thursday before the Crusade, which started on Sunday, the Crusade workers came to town. I was chairing a large luncheon for them, sponsored by the Chamber of Commerce and the Rotary Club, at the Camelot Hotel. It was a sell-out of over 800 tickets. All the singers and pianist were to perform including George Beverly Shea singing "How Great Thou Art."

I had been told that Billy Graham could not attend as they tried to save his strength for the Crusade. I begged Buddy Sutton to just let him walk in and down the aisle, across the stage and let people get a closer look at him. Then he could leave without saying one word. That would satisfy the people to get a close-up look. I was in the middle of introducing the head table, which had every constitutional officer of the State present, when Buddy and Billy Graham walked in the door. The crowd went wild. He walked down the middle aisle and onto the platform and stopped by me.

I said, "When I was profiled in the *Arkansas Democrat* several years ago, they asked me who I would rather meet than anyone else on earth—dead or alive. Not knowing you would ever come to Little Rock, I said, 'Billy Graham' and here you are." He laughed real big, put his arms around me and gave me a big bear hug. He gave a few words of greeting and then left.

In one of the pictures taken that day, it shows me talking with Billy Graham looking at me and listening. One of my children said, "Even

Billy Graham listens when Mother talks." My cousin Eloise, who had worked with the Billy Graham Crusade, said she had never known him to hug a woman before. I guess he could tell I was perfectly harmless.

My entire family came that first Sunday night. Teddy and Debbie from Memphis. Vikki and her family from Poplar Bluff. Janie and her family. Teddy and Debbie went forward to re-dedicate their lives to the Lord.

On Monday night, I was asked to give the opening prayer. Each night, one of the committee members was asked to voice the opening prayer. I considered it a real honor. I was allowed three minutes. I sat on the platform with Billy Graham and his entire group. Governor Bill Clinton sat next to me. Needless to say, I was nervous but the Lord helped me and I stayed within my three minutes.

It was a glorious week. My husband and I sang in the choir each night. Of all my activities, this was probably the most rewarding.

Crusade Prayer

Monday, September 18, 1989

DEAR FATHER, we want to thank You for giving Little Rock, Arkansas the privilege of lifting up the name of Jesus! We want to thank You for bringing your "Warrior" Billy Graham, to us to proclaim the good news of salvation! We want to thank You for the area churches with their pastors and laymen who pulled together with work and study and prayer for this crusade. We want to thank You for the business leaders who gave of their time and effort and expertise for this cause. But, most of all we want to thank You for the hundreds of prayer partners who filled in the blanks of their "Operation Andrew" and "Triplet" folders with the names of their loved ones and friends who they are burdened for. And, Lord, you know they have prayed over these names for months and wept over them until the ink has run! And, we know with your all-knowing power you are aware of every name on every list of every partner! And now, Lord, we ask You tonight to lay Your hands on each and every name and then turn Your Holy Spirit loose on 'em—with convicting power! Until grown men will fall on their knees in the market place...and mothers in the kitchen...and students in the classroom...and farmers in the fields...and people will show up here this week in this stadium—who had sworn they wouldn't come—all because of your convicting power and your promise that You will honor the prayers of the righteous and Your message that Jesus is the Answer! And for this we will give You all the credit and praise and honor and glory forever. And we ask it all in the precious name of Jesus. Amen.

Volunteering

I HAVE BEEN A VOLUNTEER ALL MY LIFE. I try to encourage others to volunteer, especially Seniors. You are never too old to volunteer. It will enrich your life.

I have always been active in my Nazarene Church. I've held just about every lay position you can except Treasurer and Janitor. I am still a lay speaker.

For 14 years I co-directed the Arkansas Junior Miss Program along with Charles Bill Black. I was also the chaperone for the state winner. To this day, the girls still call me "Mama Krutz." It's a very prestigious program for only 12th grade girls. They must have at least a B grade average, be an active volunteer, and be talented. During my fourteen years, Arkansas had three national America's Junior Miss winners— the only state in the nation to ever do this. Mr. Black was a wonderful director.

Jane receiving the National Chamber of Commerce Award in Washington, D.C. in 1986 for selling more local Chamber of Commerce memberships than anyone in the nation. Her record has never been broken.

When I was asked to direct the first drive against Cerebral Palsy in Arkansas, I was scared to death. I had volunteered in other fundraisers but never directed one. I was absolutely petrified. I was told to ask Willie Oates for help. Although it was our first meeting, she took me under her wing. She gave me all her books and records and showed me what to do. Willie and I remained close friends until her death.

I'm probably the first woman elected PTA president before her first child entered the First Grade. I made the mistake at a summer meeting, before Teddy started school, of telling the ladies how I thought some things should be run. They immediately elected me President. That should have taught me a lesson. But no, I continue to mouth off at meetings and end up being elected President. I will go into a meeting determined to sit in the back, keep my mouth shut, just listen, and not get involved. But before it is over, I'm up front telling them what to do. That's the reason Ted had the business card printed "Jane Krutz, General Manager of the Universe." He said I'm the only person who thinks I can run everything.

General Manager of the Universe

JANE KRUTZ

501-375-5209 BUS.
501-663-5437 HOME

501-227-4889 JANIE
314-686-4645 VIKKI

Jane and President Bill Clinton

My work with the Salvation Army has been very rewarding. I've served as President of the Women's Auxiliary and two terms as First Vice President of the Advisory Board. I'm still active in the auxiliary and the Board. I speak often for their conferences.

When I was named one of the Top 100 Women in Arkansas at the awards luncheon, they seated me at the table with Mrs. Helen Walton. I was bragging about this to a friend. She said, "Jane, they were just trying to equalize the wealth at the table."

Staying busy for worthwhile causes has certainly kept my life singing.

*Governor Mike Huckabee presents Jane
with her Certificate as Arkansas Mother of the Year 2000.*

*Jane celebrates winning the
Greater Little Rock Chamber
of Commerce Sales Award.*

Mrs. Senior Central Arkansas 1990

Jane (age 16) with Don Ameche at Universal Studios in 1942

Over Achiever

I HAVE A FAULT OF CHARACTER. Anything I do, I have to do more than anyone. I'm one of those obnoxious over achievers. I had to sell more Girl Scout cookies than anyone or more American Legion poppies. Being competitive is a good thing, but I was ridiculous. Of course, it's how I kept my office buildings 100% full for forty years.

It's no wonder when I fell in love with the movie star Don Ameche at the age of thirteen, that I saved hundreds of his pictures and everyone was aware of my love for him. When I was sixteen and on a trip to California, I met him and was his guest at the Universal Studios where he was filming a picture with Loretta Young and Brian Ahern. I was declared the world's #1 Don Ameche Fan and my picture appeared with him in the *Arkansas Democrat* and several fan magazines. In later years, I interviewed him by phone during the Ray Nielsen's *Good Times Picture Show* program on AETN. Don Ameche and I kept in touch until he died at the age of 83. Because of my volunteer work on PBS, I met many other famous people.

Jane and Ray Nielsen

CHAPTER 10

Aggressiveness

Jane makes a point regarding PBS.

II CORINTHIANS 3:12

Aggressiveness

Let me call you "Sugar."

A NEWSPAPER REPORTER once referred to me as a "pushy broad." Being aggressive is one of my character faults. But it's taken me a few places I could not have gone otherwise.

While working with the Junior Miss program, I went to Mobile, Alabama for the national pageant. Lorne Greene ("Bonanza") was the guest emcee. I arrived at the auditorium during rehearsals. All the girls and Mr. Greene were on the stage. I wanted to let our Arkansas contestant, Rosemary Dunaway, know that I was there. I also wanted to meet Mr. Greene.

I was not aware that the directors from all the states had been told that no one was allowed on stage during rehearsals except the girls and Mr. Greene. I started up the steps to the stage. About halfway up, a guard stopped me and asked me where I was going. I laughed and said, "Why, up on the stage."

He said, "Who are you?"

I said, rather curtly, "Why I'm Mrs. Krutz. Who do you think I am?"

"Oh, Mrs. Krutz, I'm sorry. Go right ahead."

I hugged Rosemary and then told Mr. Greene how pleased we were to have him emcee the show. We had a nice conversation. After I came down, I found out Charles Black, our director, nearly had a heart attack in the balcony when he was watching what I was doing. He was afraid they would disqualify Rosemary because I broke the rules. But she went on that night to win the national title.

Another thing happened that week in Mobile, on the final night after the pageant was over, there was a big reception. It was jam-packed—almost like sardines. I had my fur jacket hung over my arm, pushing my way through the crowd, when a man next to me yelled, "Stop, lady, stop!"

I stopped and said, "Why?"

It turned out that the hook on my fur coat had somehow hooked into the pull on his pants zipper and I was unzipping his pants as I walked. It took three people working hard to get the hook out of the hole. The room full of people were laughing hysterically by the time we got untangled.

Oh well, all's well that ends well.

She Calls Everybody "Darling"

I WENT WITH A GROUP of women to Washington, D.C. in 1976 to attend the President's Prayer Breakfast. One of our group was a close friend to Mrs. John McClellan and we were invited to the 80th birthday party for her husband, U.S. Senator John McClellan from Arkansas. It

Jane and her best friends Dorothy Mills and Hilda Thevenet greet Senator John McClellan at his 80th birthday party in Washington, D.C. in 1976.

took a couple of days for us to get clearance from the Secret Service to attend—but we passed.

Everybody who was anybody was there—every U.S. Senator, Congressman, Four-Star General, Navy Admiral, etc. We were able to mingle with them and have photos taken. I had a long conversation with Senator Hubert Humphrey.

Suddenly, President Gerald Ford walked in surrounded by Secret Service men. I've never seen eyes like these men had. They darted back and forth, seeming to look everywhere at once. No smile on any of their faces.

We were each allowed to shake the President's hand, speak to him, and have a photo taken with him. He was so personable and put everyone at ease. So much so, that when it was my turn I said, "Why, Sugar, you are better looking in person than you are in pictures." He laughed real loud.

The Secret Service man closest to me grabbed my two arms above the elbows and said, "Did you call the President "Sugar"? I was shocked and frightened. I said, "Well, I did not aim to but I'm so bad about that."

President Ford said, "Leave her alone. She's okay." With that, the man turned me loose but did not smile. I guess the President knew I was harmless.

The habit of calling everyone endearing names like "Darling," "Sugar," "Honey," "Angel," and "Sweety" is a trait of my family. I grew up hearing my mother and all her brothers and sisters use those names. Even to strangers, waiters, and clerks. So it just comes naturally to me.

Of course, my husband said the reason I call everyone "Darling" is because I can't remember anyone's name.

Walter Pidgeon

IN 1958 when I was directing the Cerebral Palsy Fund-raiser I had gone to the main Post Office to pick up mail. Coming out, I was looking down at the mail and bumped head on into a man. I looked up into the eyes of Walter Pidgeon. He was in Little Rock for one night in a play at Robinson Auditorium. His picture was on the front page of the morning newspaper so I recognized him immediately. We both jumped back and laughed. I said, "Mr. Pidgeon, how wonderful to have you visit Little Rock. I'm Jane Krutz and I'm so proud to meet you."

He asked what I was doing. I explained that I was on my way to pick up my three children from school and take them back to my office.

He asked if he could ride with me to see a little of the city. I was thrilled to do this. But, first, I had to put a towel over the hole in the front seat of my car. We laughed about that. He said he was met at the airplane by the mayor, given a key to the city, taken to the Marion Hotel and dropped off. He had nothing else to do all day until show time and wanted to see Central High School, as he had seen the news about it. He also wanted to see a Southern Baptist Church as his mother had been a Southern Baptist.

I took him to the Immanual Baptist Church, to Central High School—which he thought was beautiful. I also drove him by all three of our State Capitols and some of the scenic places in town. I explained my children would not realize how famous he was as it had been a few years since he had made movies. He said he understood that. But, I told him they would understand when I tell them he was more famous than Don Ameche. They had grown up hearing about Don Ameche and seeing my pictures with him. I picked up the two girls at Garland Elementary and Teddy at West Side Junior High. They were all giggles when they realized we had a famous movie star in the car with us.

He asked if I would have dinner with him before the show. Of course, I accepted. Ted was traveling and I knew he would be happy for me to do this. We took the children to the Cerebral Palsy office where volunteers were working. They all came out to the car and met Mr. Pidgeon and got autographs.

I left the children in their care to stuff envelopes while I went to dinner. We walked into the front door of the old Marion Hotel and turned to the right to go into the dining room. Mr. Pidgeon said, "I can't go into the dining room. I would never get through my meal. We have to eat in my room."

"That's fine. I understand."

So, up to his room we went. His manager was in an adjoining room and came in to meet me. We ordered off the room service menu. I ordered a BLT and ice tea. Mother always said you can't go wrong with a BLT, especially if you're nervous. And I was nervous.

We had a great conversation about our families, work, etc. He offered to get tickets for me and the children for the play that night but I had scheduled a large group of volunteers to come in to work and could not leave them. I always regretted that we did not go to the play and did not have a camera.

When I got up to leave he took my hand and said, "You have treated me like a normal human today. Usually, people treat me with 'awe' and are uncomfortable. You will never know how I appreciate this day."

I called Ted and everyone I could think of to tell them about the experience. My Uncle Walter Parker said, "Weren't you afraid someone would see you going into that hotel room with a man?"

"If I had known ahead of time, I would have had TV cameras there."

Oh, well, some times it pays to be a "pushy broad."

CHAPTER 11

Senior Years

This speech has been my most requested. I have given it to Senior groups across the nation—from Schroon Lake, New York to Pasadena, California to Orlando Florida and all points in between. The two remarks I hear most often after the speech are:

"I wish my mother-in-law could hear this."

"I wish I had heard this when I was younger."

PROVERBS 16:31

Enjoy Your Senior Years

Growing old gracefully

I WAS BORN THE ONLY CHILD of Fannie and Victor Gray. Mother and Daddy were both great musicians. They were born with talent. Mother could play a piano from the time she could crawl up on a piano stool and she sang high soprano. Papa sang bass. He was a choir director back in the days before we had ministers of music. He was just an old-fashioned choir director. He sang bass in quartets and was the president of the Arkansas Gospel Music Association for many years. They gave their talent to the Lord and sang for the church and revival meetings.

They just knew that their only little chicken would inherit their musical talent. From the time I was six years old, Mother had me under a piano and voice teacher. By the time I was twelve years old, I had run through five teachers. The last one finally leveled with Mother and said,

"Mrs. Gray, Jane did not inherit your and Mr. Gray's musical talent. She just didn't get it. She will never learn to play the piano and she will never sing pretty. Loud, maybe. But not pretty. The only God-given gift that child received was talking. She does that a lot. You need to find a good speech teacher and put her over Jane. Maybe she can guide that mouth of hers to some productive use in life because she will be talking until she dies."

Mother found Mrs. Allen and she began taking me around, from the time I was 13, to all the Senior citizen groups in Little Rock. The Woman's City Club. The Eastern Star. Every Senior Sunday school class of every denomination in Little Rock. I was ecumenical before ecumenical was cool. She took me to the Senior classes, she said, because I was just getting started and was a little nervous. I might mess up and the Seniors wouldn't remember it.

I walked into those Sunday school classes and looked around at all those little blue-haired ladies and those bald-headed men in their SAS oxfords. I wondered, "How on earth did they get that old?"

Well I'm one now and I'm still talking to Seniors all over the country because I have a message for them.

Your Senior years can be some of the best years of your life if you allow them to be. That's the secret. You have got to allow them to be. Aging is a state of mind. You need to face it. There is not one thing you can do about it. It happens and isn't even your fault. You don't even have to feel guilty about it. The wrinkles. The age spots. The hammer toes. They are just part of the process of aging and you don't need to get upset about it. There is no way in the world that you can turn the clock back no matter how hard you try. But you can wind it up again!

I loved all the stages of my life. I was a happy child. I was a very happy teenager. At the age of 16 I met my pretty soldier in 1942 at

Camp Robinson. We married when I was 17 and I was the happiest wife in the world. There never was a happier married woman than I was. We had three children—a son and two daughters. I was a happy mother. I even thought PTA was fun. I did the Scout work and Little League, and loved it all.

After our children were grown, I became more involved in my career as a property manager and building manager. I loved that through the years. I worked until I was 75 because I loved my work and it allowed me to get out and do other things I like to do. But the greatest season of my life is *now* because I am a grandmother. I have seven grandchildren and six great-grandchildren. Being a grandmother is the greatest thing in the world and many of you know that.

My husband would travel with me on my speaking trips if we could drive instead of fly. He said this was biblical because the Bible says, "Lo, I will be with you always." It doesn't say one word about "high," he refused to fly. When I have to fly somewhere, I always have a grandchild at the right age to go with me. They're able to take time off from school and they'll say, "It's my turn, Grandma. I want to go with you."

In 1995 I flew to Washington to speak about PBS funding. Congress was trying to take away the money from PBS. I told them we had to have something decent to watch on TV and that they better keep the money with PBS, which they did. On that trip, I took my granddaughter Jennifer with me.

Ted said, "Jane, you can't afford to take Jennifer. You'll have to buy her ticket and you're taking her out of school. You'll have to pay her way. You can't afford that."

"You're right. I really can't. When I die I won't leave one dime for those children, but they're going to say, 'Wasn't Grandma fun!' I would rather have them remember me that way than with some CD in a lock box."

Jane and family

*Jane and Ted with
granddaughter Sarah Jane*

*Grandchildren Victor and Sarah Jane
(Janie's son and daughter)*

Jane with grandsons Kyle and Jon (Teddy's sons)

Grandsons Ben and Jake
(Vikki's sons)

Granddaughter Jennifer
(Vikki's daughter)

Refrigerator Wisdom

Do you have a refrigerator that you can read? I do. Every time I find something profound, wonderful, or cute I stick it on the refrigerator. You can tell by looking at me that I spend lots of time around the refrigerator. Here are a few quotes from my refrigerator:

This poem gives you an idea about how my grandkids feel about me...

In the dim and distant past when the tempo wasn't fast,
Grandma used to rock and knit, crochet, tat, and baby-sat.
When the kids were in a jam, they could always count on Gram.
In the age of glorious living, Grandma was the gal for giving.
Grandma, now, is in the gym exercising to stay slim.
She's off touring with the bunch, taking clients out to lunch.
She's in the beauty shop, her hair to curl.
All her days are in a whirl.
Nothing seems to stop our blocker.
Now that Grandma's off her rocker.

You determine and make the choice of whether you are going to enjoy these Senior years or whether you're not. It is strictly up to you.

Another quote says,
Happy people have decided to be happy.
Miserable people have decided to be miserable.

If you don't believe it, just try it. You better try hard, because other people will not want to be around you if you are miserable. I read a quote by a lady who was 100 years old who said, "Life is short. It's up to you to make it sweet."

Great Grandchildren Ashley and Eric
(Jon's daughter and son)

Great Grandchildren
Patrick and Jonathan
(Jennifer's sons)

Great Grandchildren Spencer and Taylor
(Kyle's son and daughter)

**REFRIGERATOR
WISDOM:**

I could be
MORE MODEST
if it weren't for my

*Awesome
Grandkids.*

There are some great perks about being old. I love the discounts. I toodle through McDonald's and tell them, "Honey, I'm old. Give me that Senior coffee." Or I go through Wendy's and say, "Darling, 10% now. Remember, I'm an old lady!" I don't mind that at all. I throw out that AARP card everywhere I go and get every discount I can get.

There's also another perk for me. In this day, I love being the age I am because I don't have to learn to use computers. I think it's wonderful for those in their 70s and 80s to learn how to use computers, but if I can't do it walking and talking, I can't do it. Remember, I'm the kid who couldn't learn to play the piano under five teachers. I look at a computer and say, "Lord, help me. All of my children have to learn to work those computers and thank you, Jesus, that I don't." I do fine with my paper and pencil. Everything isn't bad about being the age we are, but it is strictly a state of mind.

Victor Diffee is a double cousin of mine. He was the ring bearer in our wedding in 1943. He once sent the following message to me and it has turned yellow with age on my refrigerator: *Old age is always fifteen years older than I am.*

But there's always a smart aleck in every bunch. I have a girlfriend who came to my house one day and saw that message on the refrigerator. She later sent this card to me in the mail that said: *Some people think life gets better as we get older. Of course, these are the same people who think professional wrestling is real.*

Some people sit at home and won't go anywhere. I asked a friend to attend a church event with me and she replied, "My arthritis hurts too much for me to sit that long in services."

"My goodness, my arthritis is so bad sometimes that if I didn't have hands and arms to help me get up out of a chair, I would just have to roll out of it onto the floor. But I am not going to let that stop me from having fun."

Another friend said that she just didn't have the money to attend. I said, "Darling, you've got more money than I have."

"I don't want to spend it. I just want to save it for my children."

Save it for my children? I encouraged mine to get a good education and make a lot more money than their daddy and me had ever made. That's not hard to do—making more money than we made. I was still working until the age of 75. I want us to be able to go have fun and do things. If folks want to make an excuse, they will make one. Then they will sit at home and complain because they are miserable and don't have anything to do, and don't have any fun in life.

FROM MY REFRIGERATOR: *Most people say when you get old you have to give things up. I say, you get old because you give things up.* Giving things up is not the thing to do.

President Bush said to just get interested in something and your life will sing. And it will. The secret is, you have to get involved in something. Even if it's just a hobby. Collect butterflies or paint birdhouses. Restring aluminum chairs. Do anything that gets you interested in something and your life will sing.

If you are looking for something to do, there is a lot of volunteer work out there. You might say, "I'm too old to volunteer." No, you are not. The greatest group of volunteers in America today are Senior citizens. There is plenty of work for you to volunteer for. In your church. In your city. The Salvation Army. Your local hospital. There are many good volunteer jobs that you can do. Get involved and you won't be bored. My husband said that I would volunteer for anything if they would brag on me. If it's a good cause, I'll volunteer for it. My mother told me when I was a child, "Jane, if you have enough food to eat, enough clothes on your back, a house to live in, and are in good health, you have to give back to the Lord for the blessings He has given you. "Give to those who have not been as blessed as you have been. Besides that, you need to realize that Jesus was the first director of the office of volunteerism.

Jesus told us that if we would feed the hungry, clothe the naked, help the sick, and visit the jails, that He will actually give us credit for doing it to Him. What better payback do you want than that? He tells us that when we do these things we become a servant of mankind. We become great in the eyes of God. What better payback do you want? As a volunteer, you also get a personal payback. You meet people. You go places. You get to do things that you wouldn't get to do if you had not volunteered. The great songs of my life have not come from leasing office buildings and selling real estate. The great music of my life has come from my volunteer efforts. I've been a volunteer for Public Broadcasting since the day it went on the air, strictly because I want my children to have some decent television to watch.

This little girl from Little Rock whose father sold used cars, whose husband sold toilet paper, and who had a high school education, would never have been able to travel to the places I've been, receive some of the awards I've been given, and meet some of the famous people I've met. I've had lunch with Captain Kangaroo at the Governor's Mansion. You just can't hardly beat that.

I've sat on the piano bench with Mark Russell, the great political satirist. I didn't play the piano, but I sat on the bench with him. That counts a little bit. I've stood at the podium with McNeil and Lehrer, the great PBS newscasters. I've stirred soup with Julia Child and shared the stage with Sherri Lewis and little Lamb Chop. I've been serenaded by the great Irish Tenors and danced The Polka with Bobby Burgess of the Lawrence Welk Show. Those things in life have made life wonderful.

FROM MY REFRIGERATOR: *I want my kids to know that if they are successful in life, they have to give back.*

Greed is not a trait to be proud of. If you are a person who is not willing to do anything for free as a volunteer, you might be called greedy and you don't want that to happen.

My mother told me when I was a little girl, "Jane, if you will wash dishes with the right attitude, it can be fun." That was the way she raised me. She lived to be 83 years old. A few years after she died, the *Arkansas Democrat* ran an article with the headline: "Attitude Makes the Difference in Older People's Lives." They had taken 100 Senior citizens and tracked them for ten years. They learned that attitude makes the difference in whether they enjoy life or not. They could have asked Fannie Gray that years ago and saved all that time and money.

If you are a grandparent, aunt, or uncle, this is important: Your attitude will determine if your own kids want to spend time with you. It will determine if your next door neighbor wants to go walking at the mall with you—or even have coffee with you. It will determine whether or not they want to sit next to you at the table.

In Little Rock, we took a lot of our Senior trips on buses. Traveling on one of our trips was a couple from our church—a born-again Christian couple. They came to church every time the doors were open. They gave their tithe. I knew they were going to Heaven. But when they went on one of our bus trips, the director had to assign a day for each one of us to eat at the table or sit with them in the pew. We loved these people. We just didn't want to sit by them. They had never eaten a meal that was fit to eat. They had never slept in a bed that was comfortable. They had never stayed in a hotel room that was clean. They had never listened to a program that was worth sitting through. It wasn't much fun sitting with people like that. They found fault like you were going to give them an award for it. I've told God I do not want to live next door to them in Heaven.

I want to say again, your attitude will determine if your grandkids will want to come see you or not. How many people do you know who say, "I never get to see my grandkids. They just run in and get their Christmas gift and never come spend time with me."

Listen to what they say when the grandkids come in. Are they complaining to them about their hair? And the clothes? Or some little faddish thing they are wearing? Are they always on them all the time about something? When my grandkids were born, I made up my mind that I was not going to fuss at them about anything as long as it was not illegal, immoral, or unethical. I was going to love them regardless of what they looked like or any of the other trivial things they will grow out of. James Dobson said, "Don't worry, honey, they'll be thirty some day."

Grandparents need to remember that. Leave the fussing to the moms and dads. They'll get enough of that. We just need to love them. We need to tell them every time they come that we love them. It doesn't matter if their clothes are grungy. It doesn't matter if they took a good pair of jeans and cut holes down them if that's what all the other kids are doing. That's not illegal, immoral, or unethical.

I have a grandson who was raised on a farm at Heber Springs, Arkansas. One day when he was sixteen, he walked into the house and he had a huge gold earring in one ear. This was not his usual style. He usually walked in with manure on his cowboy boots. He was not a kid you would expect to see wearing a gold earring. I didn't say a word. I just hugged him and kissed him and asked him about his girlfriend. In a minute, he got right up in my face and wiggled that earring. I didn't say a word and just started talking faster and loving him more. In a minute, he got up so close that he hit my nose with that earring. I didn't say a word. I just talked faster. In a minute, he said, "Grandma, how do you like my earring?"

"Oh, that's wonderful, honey."

"So you like it?"

"No. I didn't say I like it. I think a boy with a big earring in his ear looks kinda goofy. But if it makes you happy, it just tickles Grandma to death."

He came a few weeks later—the earring was gone and the hole had grown together. Later, he completed four years in the Marine helicopter service. But I believe if I had ragged that boy about the earring, it would still be there today.

I have another grandson named Jacob. He could take the prize for growing hair. He can shave off a beard today and two weeks later have a full beard. Same thing with his hair. He decided a few years ago that he was going to try every style in the world for hair and a beard. One time it would be to his shoulders. The next time it would be in a curly Afro. The next time it would be shaved in a Mohawk. A ponytail. Shaved like a billiard ball. He did the same thing with his beard. He would have a long one down on his chest. An Abraham Lincoln beard. Goatee. Handlebar moustache that curled up on the ends. His mother said to me, "Mother, would you please talk to Jacob about his hair and beard? He's driving us crazy."

"You think I'm going to fuss at Jacob? That boy makes straight As in school, he has never been in trouble one minute of his life, and he calls me his Beauty Queen. Do you think I'm going to fuss at him about anything?"

That boy loves his Grandma and loves to visit and spend time with me because all I do is love him when he's here.

You better be careful how you treat your kids and grandkids because they are the ones who will choose the nursing home for you.

Attitude. If you have a problem with your attitude, you better work on it or you will end up a lonely old person.

FROM MY REFRIGERATOR: *Act enthusiastic and you will be enthusiastic.*

Don't you just love to walk up to someone and say, "Hi, Honey, how are you?"

"Oh. Just fine."

"You sick or something?"

"No. No, I'm just fine."

Well, you're going to look them up next time, aren't you?

Do you know that Senior citizens sometimes have the problem of getting where we aren't enthusiastic when people talk to us? We ought to be so tickled that anybody would pay us any attention, especially young people. If they even walk up to us and speak, we ought to look them in the eye, talk to them, and act thrilled that they would even pay us any attention. You need to work on your enthusism because you will generate interest in yourself and have friends. People will be swarming around you if you're enthusiastic enough.

"I feel fine."

MY MOTHER AND FATHER were married 63 years when he died at the age of 80. I sold Mother's home in North Little Rock and moved her to Little Rock within a few blocks of me, into a high-rise apartment for widows. I told her when I moved her in, "Now, Mama, I know you and Daddy have been inseparable for 63 years and this is going to be hard on you. It's going to be hard on me because I was a 'daddy's girl' and we can just lay and cry all we want to, but I don't want you walking down into the vestibule of that home with all the other widows and crying and whining over Daddy. I don't want you walking in there and saying, 'Oh, I'm so lonesome! Oh, I miss Victor! Oh, I'm a widow! Oh, I don't know how I'm going to make it!' There's not a woman in there who had a husband 63 years like you had. They won't like you if you walk down there whining and crying all the time. I don't want to hear that you've gone down in that vestibule and whined and cried over Daddy. And, another thing, while we're talking about it—I want you to learn right now that the greatest four-letter word in the world, outside of love, is fine. F-I-N-E. As in, 'Hello, how are you? Oh, I'm just fine.' Now that is what I want you to learn to say any time anyone asks you how you are. Down here in Arkansas, when people say, 'How are you?' they are merely saying, 'Howdy-do.' They are not interested in how you are. Only close friends and relatives are interested. They do not want to know that your arthritis is hurting you today. They don't care of one of the grandkids is flunking in school. They are not interested in how low the rate has gone on your CD. In fact, they may not care of you had to take ex-lax® last night. I want you to say, 'Just fine.'"

"Well, Darling, I'd be lying if I said I feel just fine when my arthritis is hurting me."

"Mother, God will be pleased with you because He tells us that we are to be content in any state we find ourselves in. He will like it if you put on a happy face and say, 'just fine.'"

When she died three years later, several of the ladies came to her funeral and one of them came up to me and said, "Jane, I want you to know that your mother was a joy to live around! She never complained. She never whined or cried about anything that was wrong. Even when we knew her arthritis was so bad that we had to help her up and down out of the chair. When we would ask her how she was, she would merely smile and say, 'just fine.' That's all we ever heard her answer. Your mother was a joy!"

"Thank you, Jesus." My mother was a witness because joy is the most infallible proof of the presence of God in your life. Joy, regardless of what you are going through. In spite of your circumstances. It makes no difference if things are good or bad when you show joy like that.

John 10:10 says that He came that we would have life and we would have it more abundantly. There is nothing abundant about an old crotchety, nagging, belly-aching, argumentative, negative Christian.

FROM MY REFRIGERATOR: Luke 7:47 says, "My soul magnifies the Lord and my spirit rejoices in God, My Saviour." You haven't magnified anything or rejoiced in anything when you are a negative person.

I'm not talking about glee. There is a difference in glee and joy. I'm talking about the joy that Jesus can give. It comes from within and wells up within you and your family sees it. That is a greater message to your children than anything you can read to them out of the Bible or talk to them about. If they see that kind of joy in their grandmother and grandfather, and the day comes that they are in that kind of trouble, they will reach for the Source of joy that they saw you reach for.

This is out of *Prime Time* magazine from years ago:

Let me grow lovely growing old.

So many fine things do.

Laces, ivory, gold, and silver

Need not be new

And there is healing in old trees

Old streets a glamour hold

Why may not I as well as these

Grow lovely, growing old.

Do not kid yourself—Seniors do have problems. Growing old is not a "piece of cake." We Seniors do have problems. If you haven't had any, you just live a little longer.

When my kids grew up and left home, I got tired of cooking. I had cooked three meals a day and fixed lunches all those years. When they were gone I told Papa, "We are going to start eating out in these cute restaurants around Little Rock that we haven't had a chance to eat in."

"Jane, you've lost your mind. You're one of the best cooks in the world."

"I know I'm a good cook, but I'm tired of it and we're going to start eating out in these restaurants."

"No other woman feels that way."

"I know they do. I've heard them talk about it. One day I found this at a gift shop and I ran home and hung this on my refrigerator: "If God wanted me to cook, why did He invent restaurants?"

I should have known I was going to have a problem when I mentioned restaurants to my husband Ted. I was married to him for 64 years. He was the prettiest man in the state of Arkansas but he was never known as the last of the big time spenders. I was married to him for twenty years before I knew the first line on every menu was not "Oh, my God!"

When the kids were little we did occasionally go out to Franke's Cafeteria after church on Sunday. We would save our money and sometimes we could take them out to eat. One Sunday, we were sitting in Franke's and there was an older couple sitting over at the next table. They kept looking at us and talking, and looking back at us and talking. I said, "Ted, why do you think they are talking about us?"

"I don't know but they sure are talking about us because they keep looking over here and then talking."

When they got up to leave, they stopped at the table and the lady said, "We just want to compliment you. Your children are the best-behaved children I've ever seen in a restaurant. All three of them (they were little at the time) have just behaved beautifully. We just think it's wonderful and we wanted to tell you."

I said, "I appreciate that. We keep trying to raise them that way."

The man said to our son who was about eleven years old at the time, "Son, does your daddy give you instructions before you come into a restaurant?"

"Oh, yes sir. All the time."

"What does he say to you?"

"Pick something cheap!"

ANOTHER THING THAT HAPPENS as we get older is that our metabolism changes and our weight gives us a problem. You would never believe that when I married Ted I had a 21-inch waistline. As I have aged, I am on a diet, or off a diet or starting a diet or talking about a diet. I invented the see-saw syndrome, gaining and losing pounds two or three times a year. I do suffer from two dread diseases that are not compatible. One is gluttony and the other is vanity. I am too big of a glutton to not eat what is in front of me and too vain to be happy when

I get too big, so I'm constantly see-sawing. I have three sets of clothes in my closet.

Of course, we Nazarenes all have a little problem with weight. The reason is we've been raised to not smoke, drink, or carouse around. The only thing they let us do is eat and they raised us on potluck dinners. Why wouldn't we have a weight problem? I was married to a smart-aleck who could still wear his World War II uniform. He had never changed five pounds through the years. I just hate people like that and they are always throwing it up to you. He came home and put this on the refrigerator: "Diet is on." When you turn it over it says, "Diet is off." He told me I needed to keep it current because he didn't know if he was supposed to bring home ice cream or cottage cheese that week.

I have found other quotes like:

"I keep trying to lose weight but it keeps finding me."

"Eat it today. Wear it tomorrow."

"I cheat on my diet."

Another reason women don't like to cook is that when our husbands retire, they become the boss in the kitchen. They want to see what is being cooked and what is going in it. Ted was a health nut before it was popular to be a health nut. He has counted cholesterol, fat grams, sugar, and salt through the years. When he was working, he wasn't home to watch what I cooked. When he retired I couldn't use any of the good stuff.

I had to be a closet cook and hide in the pantry if I added salt or sugar or butter. I told him all he was going to get out of this was two more years in a nursing home. Sometimes he would say he didn't know why the Lord did not take him on to Heaven and I told him if he quit taking all those vitamins and minerals, the Lord might do it.

Bathroom Humor

ANOTHER THING THAT BOTHERS US—when I was young, I was ruled by my heart. As I got older and wiser, I was ruled by my head. Now my bladder rules everything. My daughter said I should get a face lift—I'm getting so wrinkled. I said, "What good would it do for me to look like Marilyn Monroe when I can't get five feet away from a restroom?"

Singleness

ANOTHER THING WOMEN are bothered with is when they lose their spouse. Now, men don't have this problem. All they have to do is pick the best casserole widows bring them and they can get married any time they want to. But women can't. There were four women sitting around the table in a retirement village. A new man walked by. The first woman said, "Are you new here?"

"Yes, I just moved in yesterday."

The second lady said, "Where from?"

"San Quentin."

The third lady asked, " What were you in for?"

"I killed my wife."

The fourth lady says, "Oh, goody! He's single."

A FRIEND AT CHURCH was widowed quite young and never dated again. She said she was not interested in another man. Then, one day she called me and said," Guess what? I got married last week."

"Well, have you known him long?"

"No, I just met him a few weeks ago."

"Is he good looking?"

"No, he's kinda homely. Clean, but homely."

"Has he got lots of money?"

"No, he just lives on Social Security."

"Well, is he young?"

"No, he's a lot older than I am."

"Why in the world would you marry a man you just met who is ugly, poor, and old?

"Jane, he can drive at night."

Here today. Gone tomorrow.

ONE OF THE THINGS that bothers us as we get older is we get forgetful. I don't mean the dreaded disease that has taken some of our friends. I mean where you have to go back upstairs to remember what you came down for. We just as well laugh about it—it's lots easier to deal with if we laugh about it.

One friend said his mind was like lightning—one bright flash and then it was gone.

FOUR COLLEGE FRIENDS decided when they graduated that they would meet back in the college town for lunch when they were 40 years old. They decided on a quaint German restaurant because the waitresses were pretty and wore low-cut blouses. At the age of 50, they met again and went to the same restaurant because the food was good and the price was right. When they were 60, they went back because the music was soft and there was no smoking. At 70, they went there because they had a handicap entrance and an elevator. At the age of 80, they decided to go there because they had never been there before.

213

A FELLOW WAS GETTING real bad about not remembering names. His wife heard of a new doctor in town who could help him and took him there. When he came out he said, "This doc is great! He's taught me some new tricks that are going to help me remember names. Thanks for taking me to him."

They were walking around the mall and ran into a friend. He told him he was having the same problem. "What's the doctor's name?"

"Uh, uh, uh—wait a minute. He taught me a trick. Name a flower."

"What?"

"Name a flower."

"Petunia?"

"No, name another one."

"Gardenia?"

"No, name another one."

"Rose?"

"Yes, Rose. That's it."

He turned to his wife. "Rose, honey, can you tell him the name of that doctor?"

Drive me crazy.

TWO OLD MAID SISTERS lived together and took turns driving. One day, Mary was driving and ran a red light. When she ran the second red light, Martha spoke up, "Mary, you have just run two red lights."

"Oh, was I driving?"

I ALWAYS HAD TO FORCE TED to go for his annual checkup. I would make the appointment and then go with him to be sure he went. One time, we went for his checkup and I stayed in the reception room while Ted went in to see the doctor.

"Hello, Ted, how are you?"

"Just wonderful, God has been so good to me."

"Well, that's nice."

"No, your really don't understand. God is special to me. He does things for me he doesn't do for anyone else. For instance, last night when I got up to go to the bathroom, God turned the light on for me and when I was finished, he turned the light off for me."

"Well, that's nice. But maybe I better talk to Jane."

I went in and the doctor said, "Hello, Jane. How are you doing?"

"Just great. God has been so good to us."

"That's what Ted says. In fact, he said when he went to the bathroom last night, God turned the light on and off for him."

"Oh, my God! He has wet in the refrigerator again!"

AFTER ALL, WE SENIORS are worth a lot.

We have silver in our hair, gold in our teeth, stones in our kidneys, lead in our feet, and gas on the stomach.

Hearing Aides

MY FAMILY HAD BEGGED for me to get hearing aides for at least two years. But, every time I priced them I figured I could say "Huh?" a little longer.

One Sunday morning, Janie was visiting church with me. Pastor Casey said, "I have a really important subject to discuss with you. Our church really needs a 'worship leader' but we just can't afford it now. Unless you are willing to pay more in tithes and offerings, we can't have one. But, we really do need a worship leader."

I leaned over to Janie and said, "My goodness, Janie, are we that broke in this church that we can't afford a 'weed-eater'?"

She started laughing real big. I said, "Now this is no laughing matter. If we are that broke, we should just close the doors and go home. Why, I've got Daddy's weed-eater. I'll just give that to them or I'll buy them a new one. This breaks my heart that we can't even afford to buy a weed-eater!"

When she told me he had said "worship leader" I started laughing as loud as she was. I went the next day and got hearing aides.

When word got around about it and we did get a worship leader, his nick-name became "weed-eater."

ONE THING I WANT TO seriously mention is the fact that we Seniors deny when we get hard of hearing. We don't mind wearing glasses but there is some kind of pride that keeps us from admitting that we can't hear. If you or your loved ones have this problem, go see about it. Hearing aids are much better now than they used to be and you miss out on so much if you can't hear. So, do go see about it.

This couple was passing through town, stopped at a service station to gas up and the attendant asked the man "You folks passing through town?"

His wife yelled real loud, "What did he say?"

"He wanted to know if we were passing through town."

"Oh!"

The attendant asked, "Where are you going?"

"To Jackson, Mississippi."

"What did he say?" yelled the wife.

"He wanted to know where we are going."

"Oh!"

"Where are you from?" the attendant asked.

"Oklahoma City."

"Oh, I used to know a woman really well from Oklahoma City. But I believe that she was the meanest, most cantankerous woman I have ever known."

"What did he say?"

"He says he thinks he knows you."

So you better get hearing aids. You don't know what they might be saying about you.

Body. Mind. Spirit.

WE HUMANS ARE MADE up of three parts. Body. Mind. Spirit. The body might get bent with age. The mind might get forgetful. But the spirit is capable of growing stronger the older we get. If we feed our spirit properly, we must feed it on the meat of the Word of God, the Living Water of Jesus Christ, the Milk and Honey of the Holy Spirit, and the Bread of Life.

If you feed your spirit properly, you can become the spiritual giant to your family—even in your old age. Your children will rise up and call you blessed, and you can point them to the Throne of God!

> *Even to your old age and gray hairs. I am He!*
> *I am He who will sustain you. I have made you.*
> *I will carry you. I will sustain you and I will rescue you.*
> ISAIAH 46:4

Jane Gray Krutz

CHAPTER 12

Good Manners

Jane at one of her many speaking engagements

GALATIANS 5:13-15

Good Manners

Sit down and listen.

THIS SPEECH WAS FIRST GIVEN to a youth group at church but the older I get, the more I realize that adults, especially Seniors, are guilty of bad manners in church. This is to encourage all people to follow the Golden Rule when you are part of the audience.

Treat other performers the way you want to be treated if you were on stage behind the microphone. Your actions can help influence others in the audience to follow the good manners rule.

Be on time. Plan to leave early enough that if you get behind a wreck or have a flat, you can still be there on time. It is rude to always be late. You're saying to other people, "My time is more important than yours."

If something unexpected happens and you are late, there is a proper way to enter. Stop at the door, look for a seat that is close and easy to get to, and take off your coat before you enter. Look straight ahead, don't look to the left or right, and do not speak or smile at anyone (it distracts them). Walk fast and sit down as quickly as possible. Don't speak to anyone sitting in your row. Immediately look at the speaker or singer with rapt attention. Others will follow your action and also look at the performer.

Give your undivided attention to anyone performing on stage. Whether it's an emcee making announcements, a singer, a musician playing an instrument, a speaker, or preacher—you should treat them the same way you would if you were one-on-one with them. Treat them, as they talk to you from the platform, the same way you would treat them if they were sitting in your living room. You would not write notes to someone, turn and talk to someone else, read a book, close your eyes, look bored, and you certainly would not text anyone. You should not do any of these things while someone is performing.

Paying attention is really Biblical. God tells us we are to love our neighbor as ourselves and if you were the one on the platform, you would especially want the audience to pay attention. And if it were your child or grandchild, you would really want everyone to be quiet and pay attention. You are supposed to treat others the same way.

And not just if they are great performers. When someone is a great speaker or singer, everyone pays attention. It's the ones who aren't so good, who are shy and frightened, who need your encouragement the most. You should pray for them as they perform and smile at them even when they hit a wrong note or make a mistake. This will encourage them to keep trying and not give up. God says we are to be an encourager and one of the best ways is to be a good listener from the audience.

Even famous entertainers say they keep their eyes on someone in the audience who looks as if they are enjoying the program and do not focus on someone who looks bored. If a famous entertainer needs encouraging, how much more does some young amateur just starting out? Be an encourager.

If it will be necessary for you to leave early, pick a seat close to an exit. Don't cause any disturbance as you leave. Look straight ahead. Don't speak to people around you. Don't wave goodbye. Just walk out as quickly and quietly as you can. If someone tries to talk to you during the performance, just smile. Do not answer or try to carry on a conversation. If necessary, put your finger over your lips and turn back to look at the performer. They will get the message. There is nothing you need to talk about that can't wait until the performance is over. And remember, if it were your child performing, you would certainly not be talking.

If you are ill or in pain or so tired you can't be a good listener, then stay home. You might discourage others from enjoying the program when they look at you.

If you sing in the choir, sit on the platform, or sit at the head table at a banquet, you can orchestrate the way the audience listens. It is very important that you do not look bored, don't fiddle with paper or notes, and don't talk to others. You should turn your body toward the performer, nod your head, and look very interested in what they are doing. This will encourage the people in the audience to listen. If possible, speak to the performer and tell them how much you enjoyed their part on the program. This will encourage them.

Remember, God commands us to love others. Good common courtesy is one way to show it.

CHAPTER 13

Black Salve,
Castor Oil,
and Depends

PROVERBS 17:22

Black Salve, Castor Oil, and Depends

Jane, take your own medicine.

I WAS VERY FORTUNATE to be so healthy most of my life. I had the usual childhood illnesses—chicken pox, measles, etc. One year, the old-fashioned seven-year itch was going around. I remember the Black Salve they put on me every night until it was gone. My only dose of castor oil was given by Aunt Lora Diffee. I was spending the night with my cousin, Sarah Elizabeth, and it was flu season. Aunt Lora believed in preventative medicine, so she lined all her children up for a dose of castor oil. She lined me up with them. To this day, when I think of it, I can still taste it. Ugh!

Though I had a few colds and one case of the flu, I was always healthy. I'm sure I inherited this trait from my father. I don't remember him ever being ill, even with a cold. If he was, he never went to bed or missed a day of work. It was only in his late 70s that he developed emphysema. Although he had quit smoking in his 40s, his early years of heaving smoking had taken its toll. He died at the age of 80 from emphysema and heart failure. The doctor said he was so strong and healthy otherwise, that had he never smoked he probably would have lived to be 100.

Mother was always fragile. She was born with a bad hip that caused her to have a slight limp. She had several serious illnesses. In her later years, she suffered from high blood pressure, arthritis, and congestive heart failure. However, she lived a very active life—played piano and sang for church, taught Sunday school, and was a very active hands-on mother and grandmother. She lived to be 83 years old. She and Daddy both had very good active minds until their last breath.

I was never sick a day when I was pregnant with all three of my children. The only problem I had was weight gain. I had never had a problem with weight until Teddy was born. I gained 72 pounds while I was pregnant and he weighed 6 lbs., 4 ozs. By the time I had gone on diets and joined spas to get the weight off, Janie came along. I gained 35 pounds and she weighed 6 lbs., 6 ozs. Then again, it was diets and exercise when Vikki came along. I gained 35 pounds and she weighed 6 lbs., 5 ozs. Although my pregnancies were easy, I had long, hard labor with all three—I'm sure it was due to the extra weight.

I was in perfect health until my 50s, when arthritis hit me in my knees. For years, it would come and go, stay for a little while, then go away for long periods of time. Dr. Barry Thompson has been my orthopedic doctor through the years.

I never knew what a Hot Flash felt like. I breezed through menopause without even realizing it. Then when I was 70 years old, I was diagnosed with uterine cancer in its early stages. Dr. Reid Henry wanted to operate the next day, but the next week I had a PBS convention to attend in New Orleans and a speech to give to the Chamber of Commerce in Destin, Florida. He let me wait a week. The surgery went well, but they suggested radiation in case the cancer had invaded the lining of the uterus. I had 25 radiation treatments, never missing a day of work. However, the radiation damaged my colon and bladder. I managed to handle it for 10 years, but the problem became so bad I was forced to have a double ostomy surgery. I was in the hospital for two weeks because I developed kidney failure. I was only home a few days, then went back to the hospital for another two weeks. Eight doctors were on the team to save me. Dr. Dean Kumpuris, Internist, said I slipped through the cracks twice and they were not sure they could pull me back through.

During that time, I was so ill I really begged God to let me die. I would turn out the light at night and pray, "Oh, God, don't let me wake up here in the morning." I told this to my doctors, my family, and my preacher. Dr. Don Casey, my pastor, said, "Jane, you need to read your own speeches."

"No, they don't work. I'm never going to give them again. If I get out of here, I'm going to burn every speech and every tape. They don't work."

One day my District Superintendent, Dr. Russell Branstetter, came to visit. After listening to me he said, "Jane, the Bible says you cannot add or subtract one day to your life. God is in charge of that."

I thought, "Well, if that's the way it is, I just might as well quit fussing about it." God brought to my mind the calling card my Vikki had passed out everywhere she went. On the card were the words of Corrie Ten Boom: "There is no pit deep enough that He is not deeper still." I began to come out of that pit of depression. God restored my desire to live, to speak, and to witness again. That was four years ago. I am now 85. My primary physician, Dr. Bruce Sanderson, and kidney specialist, Dr. James Wellon, keep a close watch over me and keep my high blood pressure in check. My arthritis is bad enough that I have to use a walker or cane. Due to the radiation treatments, I have suffered cracked bones in my hip area. I live with both a colostomy and urostomy, but I'm still able to drive and travel. I speak often, appear on television regularly, serve on several boards, volunteer, and stay very active. I've been able to stay in my home with the help of an electric chair on my stairs.

Although I pray for healing, maybe God does not choose to heal my pain. Maybe He wants me to show others how to live with it. I speak often to cancer survivor groups to encourage them. To God be the Glory!

ONE DAY, WHEN TRAVELING WITH TED, the words to a song came to me and I wrote them down. Later, I started singing this song to encourage others who had the same problem (To the tune of *Thank Heaven for Little Girls*).

Thank Heaven for my Depends® and Serenity® Guards
    and even Maxithins®.
What would I do without them?
Huh. I've have to stay home and look at only him.
I'm cancer-free because of radiation.
But they zapped me through that part of my creation.
Thank Heaven for my Depends.

No one will ever know though they cost me lots of dough,
But without them what would cancer survivors do?
They keep me safe and dry no matter whether
I'm wearing silk and lace or even leather.
Thank Heaven for my Depends.
I'm hoping that some day, Medicare will agree to pay.
For without them, what would cancer survivors do?

Vikki Kreulen

"There is no pit so deep that
He is not deeper still."
Corrie Ten Boom

CHAPTER 14

Ecumenical

Jane and her pastor Dr. Dan Casey

HEBREWS 10:23-25

Ecumenical

Get to know your heavenly neighbors

THE FIRST PLACE I WAS TAKEN AFTER BEING BORN at home was the First Church of the Nazarene in Conway, Arkansas. We moved to Little Rock when I was four and lived across the street from the big First Church of the Nazarene on the corner of 9th and Battery. My aunt, Reverend Agnes White Diffee, was the pastor there for 18 years. It was the largest Nazarene Church in the Nation. One reason for our popularity was the daily radio program.

When I was nine years old I was saved at the altar during a revival meeting, baptized, and joined the church. The last place I plan to be taken before I'm buried in the Vilonia Cemetery is the Little Rock First Church of the Nazarene.

My Grandfather Gray was a Nazarene preacher. I'm a fourth-generation Nazarene. It is a good, solid Bible-teaching doctrine and has never been watered down through the years.

In case you don't know, the Nazarene Church was founded by a Methodist Bishop, Phineas F. Bresee, in Los Angeles, California in 1908. The doctrine is old-fashioned John Wesley Methodist Holiness doctrine. It is the same doctrine as the Salvation Army and the General Baptist Church, among others. We are not charismatic, but we do preach Holiness.

Some of the Rules and practices have changed through the years, but not the doctrine. In the early days, women did not wear trousers, makeup, or much jewelry. That is all acceptable today. Also, movies or mixed swimming were not allowed. Today we do teach against R-rated movies and television. We also still teach against alcohol and tobacco.

Although I was born Nazarene and plan to die Nazarene, I'm glad I was raised to have great respect for other denominations and not to think Nazarenes are the only good Christians.

I started learning this at an early age. My pastor, Aunt Agnes Diffee, would invite other churches in town to participate in the radio programs. If they were having a revival, she would invite their evangelist and revival singers to appear on the radio. This made her very respected by all the local pastors and it helped me understand that other churches had good Christians in them.

In later years I belonged to several groups that had women members from many other churches: Christian Women's Club, Salvation Army Auxiliary, Bible Study Fellowship, Community Bible Study, Baptist Senior Group, and Prison Ministries, among others. Some of the most devoted praying Christian women I ever met were in these groups. Their friendships added much joy to my life and helped strengthen my faith.

Someone asked me why I belonged to a Baptist Senior Group. I said, "If I'm going to spend eternity with these folks in Heaven, I want to get to know them down here."

I've loved every pastor I ever had and have never cast a "no" vote against one. I'm a great believer in the Scripture that says, "Touch not God's anointed." If God called them to preach, who am I to question it. And if they are not living in God's will, God will take care of it.

I've been blessed with some of the finest pastors the Church of the Nazarene has. The ones I have been the closest to, besides my Aunt Agnes and my present pastor Dan Casey, were Tom Herman, Gary Powell, Bud Scott, Ponder Gilliland, and Ron McCormick.

I've also had the privilege of knowing many of the leading Nazarene evangelists. When I was young, evangelists stayed in the home of the pastors or a church member. Since we lived across the street from the parsonage I saw those evangelists every day. The singers often stayed in our home. Some of the great ones included Tostie, Bona Fleming, Uncle Bud Robinson, Nettie Miller, Fuget, Roy Williams, and J.B. Chapman to name a few.

I also knew some of the top gospel singers because my church brought them to Little Rock for revival meetings: The Gaithers, The Statesmen, The Speer Family, The Goodman Family, the Blackwood Brothers, to name a few. The Blackwood Brothers ate many a meal at our dining room table. We became special friends with Bill Lyle. Oh, what a heritage!

I'm so glad I learned at an early age that as long as a person loves God and is saved by the blood of Jesus Christ, it does not matter where they go to church.

CHAPTER 15

The Legend of God's Trees

When in my late teens, Mrs. Allen gave me this piece, "The Legend of God's Trees," to learn for a Christmas program. The author is unknown. I started receiving requests to present it to churches and different clubs around the state. From age 17 to 85, I have never missed a December giving it to some group.

Some groups have me back year after year.

One December I was booked 16 times. I have also given this on TV shows. Though the story has been published in book form, I know of no one else who performs it. It has become my signature piece.

The message is worth repeating.

JEREMIAH 29:11

The Legend of God's Trees

God has a plan for your life.

ONCE UP ON A TIME, there was a forest of trees. Little ones. Big ones. All growing together on the hillside. In summer, they laughed in the warm sunlight. When autumn came, wrapping their limbs with beautiful leaves, they rejoiced in the beautiful colors. When winter wrapped snow about their bare limbs, they rejoiced in the beauty of this.

The trees were very happy with life just as it was on the hillside, but sometimes they spoke of things they would like to be and do when they grew up—just like children.

One little tree said, "You know, I think I would like to be a baby's cradle. I've seen people coming into the forest carrying babies in their arms. I think a baby is the sweetest thing I ever saw. When I am older, I would like to be made into a bed for a baby."

"Ha! I want to be made into something more important than that," said the second little tree. "I want to be made into a great ship and I want to sail on the water. And I want to be loaded with cargos of gold, silver, and precious jewels."

The mother tree nearby said, "I hope your wish will not bring you sorrow. And what would you like to be," she asked the third little tree. "Have you no dreams for the future?"

"No dreams. Just to stand on a hill and point to God. What can a tree do better than that?"

"What indeed, "said the mother tree, proudly.

The days went by. Weeks and months and years followed. The little trees grew up. One day some men came into the forest to cut down the first little tree. "Finally. Now perhaps I shall be made into a baby's cradle. I've waited so long."

But he was not made into a cradle at all. Instead, he was hewn into rough pieces and carelessly put together to form a manger in a stable in Bethlehem. "Oh, this is terrible," he cried. "This is not what I planned to be—shoved into a dark stable with no one to see me but the cattle. This is awful! I wish I were back in the forest."

But God, who loves little trees, whispered, "Wait and I'll show you something." And He did.

There were shepherds abiding in the field, keeping watch over their flock by night. And, lo, the angel of the Lord came upon them. And the glory of the Lord shown round about them and they were so afraid. But the angel said unto them, "Fear not. For I bring you good news of great joy which will be to all people. For unto you is born this day, in the city of David, a Savior, which is Christ the Lord. And this shall be a sign unto you: You shall find the babe wrapped in swaddling clothes lying in a manger."

As the angels went away from them into Heaven, the shepherds said to one another, "Let us go into Bethlehem and see this thing which the Lord has made known unto us."

And they came with haste and found Mary, and Joseph, and the baby lying in a manger. Yes, it was that little manger. In the stillness of the night, God had come down to lay his very *own* little baby there. This baby was the Son of God. The little manger quivered with delight. "Oh, this is wonderful," he thought. "In all my dreams, I never thought I would hold a baby like this. This is better than all my planning." All the trees on the hillside rejoiced because their little brother, the manger, had his wish come true.

Years passed, and some men came into the forest to cut down the second little tree.

"Well, finally! Perhaps now I can do all the great things which I've been planning. But he was not made into a great vessel. Instead, he was made into a tiny fishing boat. He fell into the hands of a simple Galilean fisherman named Peter. He was very disappointed.

One day he was on the shores of the Lake of Gennesaret and pondered while Peter was washing his nets.

"To think that my life has turned out like this—just a fishing boat! Peter is not even a good fisherman! He has worked all night and hasn't caught a thing. This is stupid! I wish I were back in the forest."

But God, who loves little trees, whispered, "Wait and I'll show you something." And He did.

From out of the crowd came a person called Jesus. He entered the little boat and sat down and taught the people. His words were of beauty and wisdom and light, and the multitudes listened—even the little fishing boat. When Jesus had finished speaking, He told Peter to launch out into the deep again and let down his nets. There were so many fish in the nets this time that the little boat trembled—not so much with the weight of the fish—as with the weight of wonder in his heart.

"This is wonderful," he thought. "In all my dreams, I never thought I would carry a cargo like this. This is better than all my big planning."

And on the hillside, all the trees once again rejoiced because their brother, the little boat, had found fulfillment.

Months passed by and some men came to the forest to cut down the third little tree—the one that wanted to just stand on a hill and point to God.

"I don't want to go into the valley," he cried. "Why can't men just leave me alone."

But they didn't leave him alone. They tore away his branches and cut deep into his very heart. They hewed him apart and put him together again in the form of a crude cross.

"This is terrible," he cried. "They are going to hang someone upon me. To think I must take part in a crucifixion. I, who only wanted to point to God. This is awful."

But God, who loves little trees, whispered, "Wait and I'll show you something." And He did.

One day, outside Jerusalem, a great multitude gathered, and in their midst was Jesus. Beside Him was the cross. As they led Him away, they laid hold of Simon of Cyrene and made him carry the cross, that he might bear it for Jesus. When they had come to the place called Calvary, there they crucified Him.

The cross shuddered beneath it's weight of agony and shame. Then, suddenly, a miracle happened. Jesus, after He had cried again with a loud voice, yielded up the Ghost. Behold, the veil of the Temple was ripped in two from the top to the bottom. The centurion, and those who were with him watching Jesus, saw the earthquake and they feared greatly saying, "Truly, this was the Son of God."

The little tree that had become a cross heard, floating down from the heavenly places, the echo of a remembered promise, "Now is the judgement of this world. Now shall the prince of this world be cast down and I, if I be lifted up from the earth, will draw all men unto Me."

And the cross began to understand. "This is wonderful," he thought. "I never thought to point to God this way. This is better than all my planning."

And so it was, for hundreds of trees have stood on the hillside through the years, but none of them have ever been able to point a man to God. Only the Cross of Calvary can do this.

This is the story of God's trees. Every one of them received its wish, but each at God's appointed time, in God's appointed way, and only through Jesus Christ.

Do you have any wishes? God will grant your heart's desire, but only through Jesus Christ. If you will invite Him into the stable of your heart, He will make of its lowly manger a cradle for the King. If you will turn over to Him the empty vessel of your life, He will fill it with such a cargo of blessings you will scarcely be able to hold it. And if you will deny yourself daily and take up your cross and follow Him, He will make of you someone who points the way to God.

The Christmas Parade

WHEN I'M ASKED TO DO A Christmas program for at least thirty minutes, I usually start the program with a couple of children's Christmas jokes. Then I tell the story about the Christmas parade. Folks get a kick out of this, especially if it's an ecumenical group.

The Christmas Parade

THE CITY was going to have a Christmas parade and invited representatives from every church to a meeting to plan what float they would like to put in the parade. During the ecumenical gathering, somebody rushed in and shouted, "The building is on fire!"

The Methodists gathered in a corner and prayed.

The Baptists cried, "Where's the water?"

The Christian Church members cried: "Save the Communion wine!"

The Christian Scientists agreed among themselves that there was NO fire.

The Fundamentalists shouted, "It's the vengeance of God!"

The Amish moved their horse and buggy to a safe distance.

The Lutherans posted a notice on the door declaring the fire was evil.

The Quakers quietly praised God for the blessings that fire brings.

The Unitarians declared it did not matter what method you used to put out the fire as long as you did not criticize any one else's method.

The Jews posted symbols on the door hoping the fire would pass over.

The Catholics passed the collection plate.

The Mormans sent two young men to knock on doors to see if they could get some help to put out the fire.

The Episcopalians formed a procession and marched out in grand style.

The Pentecostals had a word of advice but no one could interpret it.

The Congregationalists shouted, "Every man for himself!"

The Seventh Day Adventists said they would be glad to help put out the fire as long as they could be finished by Saturday.

The Presbyterians appointed a chairperson, who was to appoint
a committee to look into the matter.
The Nazarenes put it to a vote for the congregation as to
who should put out the fire.
The Church of Christ complained that the fire was probably caused
by a short in the electric organ.
And all the while, the Salvation Army served coffee and doughnuts.

Then, I get serious and tell the story of God's Trees. Afterwards, I
end with the following Christmas wish.

*May Christmas bring to you it's blazing hearth fires, the laughter
of little children, and at least one note of the song the angels
sang. And for the New Year, what can I wish for you? Nothing
better than those things I most wish for myself. Nothing that
would make the world or others poorer. Nothing at the expense
of other men. But just those few things which, in their coming, do
not stop with me but touch me rather as they pass and gather
strength. A few friends who understand me and yet remain my
friends. A work to do which has real value without which the
world would be the poorer. A return for such work small enough
not to tax unduly anyone who pays. An understanding heart,
a sight of the eternal hills, the unresting sea, and something
beautiful the hand of man has made. A little leisure with
nothing to do. And the patience to wait for the coming of these
things, with the wisdom to know them when they come.*

CHAPTER 16

Have You Seen Mary's Boy?

I got the idea for this speech from a sermon by Pastor Toy Arnett of the Faith Assembly Christian Church in Destin, Florida. I also want to thank him and his wife, Rena, for being such wonderful pastors to my son Teddy and his wife Debbie.

LUKE 2:19

Have You Seen Mary's Boy?

Be about your Father's business.

HE IS ABOUT TWELVE YEARS OLD. He came with His parents to Passover and when they left to go home they each thought the other had Him. But when they stopped for the night, he was not with either one and they could not find Him.

Have you seen Mary's boy? After three days of searching and nearly losing their minds, someone said, "Yes, we saw Him at the Temple. He was surrounded by teachers and scholars and they were hanging on to every word He said." When His parents arrived at the Temple and found Him they said, "Jesus, why have you done this to us? We've been frantic!" Jesus said, "But Mother and Daddy, don't you know that I must be about my Father's business?"

When I read this, the question came to my mind—"What was the Father's business Jesus had to be about?"

We don't know much about Jesus for the next eighteen years. The Bible picks up again when He is thirty. At that time if someone asked, "Have you seen Mary's boy?" the answer might been, "Yes, at the Pool of Bethesda. There was a lame man there. He had been crippled 38 years and was not able to get to the pool before others to receive healing from the stirring of the water."

Jesus looked and saw his problem. He asked, "Would you be made whole?"

"I can't. Others get to the pool first."

"Get up. Pick up your bed and go home."

Have you seen Mary's boy?

"Yes, there was a woman accused of adultery. In fact, she had been caught in the very act. They brought her to Jesus to see what He would do. They usually stoned a woman to death for this sin. Jesus said, 'He who is without sin can cast the first stone.' They all left. Jesus said, 'Woman, where are your accusers?" She said, 'They are gone.' Jesus said, 'Neither do I condemn you.'" Jesus did not come to condemn, but to seek and save the lost.

Have you seen Mary's boy?

Yes, He was walking down the road. The tax collector was a little short man named Zacchaeus and he wanted to see Jesus so badly, he climbed a tree so he could look down and see Jesus as He passed. Jesus stopped, looked up, and said, "Zacchaeus, you come down. I'm going to your house to eat." Jesus is always found by those who are looking for Him.

You'll notice Mary's boy was always found around the rejected. Sad. Hurting. Castaways. He did not surround Himself with the wealthy or popular. He was always with those who needed help.

Have you seen Mary's boy?

Yes. Again, there was a big crowd. They stayed so long to listen to His teaching, they were hungry and needed food. Jesus told his disciples, "Feed them."

"How?"

"With what you have."

The only thing they had was one little boy's lunch with a few fish and loaves of bread. After Jesus blessed it, they were able to feed over 5000 people. Jesus only expects us to use what we have for His work.

Have you seen Mary's boy?

Jesus was always where He was needed. What the Father's business really involves is loving and meeting the needs of people.

Jesus did not come to condemn, criticize, put down, or find fault. No negativity. He came with words of encouragement and concern and compassion. But, most of all, with love.

Have you seen Mary's boy?

He is seen everywhere where people are hurting or in need. He was seen at the Tomb of Lazarus. At the bedside of Jarius' daughter. In a boat when men could find no fish. In another boat when the storm came up.

Have you seen Mary's boy?

Yes, on a mountainside. Teaching great multitudes how to live a blessed life. Spreading mud on a blind man's eyes. Healing lepers. A woman of the street came into Simon's house asking to see Jesus. Simon pointed his finger and said, "That woman is a sinner, Jesus. You don't want to have anything to do with her." Jesus said, "Just a minute, Simon. I've got something to say to you. When I came into your home, you did not offer to wash my feet, as is the custom. But this woman washed my feet with her tears, dried them with her hair, and anointed them with an expensive perfume she could not afford." Jesus turned to the woman and said, "Though your sins are many, they are all forgiven."

Do you really know what the Father's business is? It is people. He went where they were. He went to parties. Sought tax collectors. Fishermen. Sat with the woman at the well. Found the ill. He was not just found in the House of Worship, but out there in the world where people are in need.

Have you seen Mary's boy?

Yes. At a wedding party. His mother pulled Jesus aside and said, "We have a problem here. The host has run out of wine and that is a disgrace. Can you help him?"

"Yes, tell my disciples I need them."

She called the disciples and said, "Do whatever He tells you to do."

They filled the empty jars with water and He turned it into wine.

He is always out there meeting needs—even trivial ones. If it's important to you, it's important to Him.

We, as followers of Jesus, need to be out there where the people are—meeting their needs.

I ask myself, "Have I really been about my Father's business? His business is loving people.

Jesus said, "Jane, you will never be able to make amends for what you have done. When you see me hanging on that cross, remember, I'm still about my Father's business. I'm your perfect sacrifice. I'm your sacrificial Lamb whose blood covers your sins.

Have you ever wondered why God, who created the whole world, did not snap His fingers and create a Bethlehem Hilton right on the spot when Jesus was to be born? God intended for Jesus to be born in a stable because that is where lambs are to be born, and He is our Sacrificial Lamb.

Have you seen Mary's boy?

"Yes, I saw Him hanging on that cross between two thieves. One was cursing Him. The other said, "Man, are you crazy? We belong here but He has done nothing to deserve this."

He turned to Jesus saying, "Will You remember me when You come into Your kingdom?"

Jesus said, "Today, You will be with Me in Paradise."

Now that goes against a lot of theology. He was not baptized. He did not take Communion. He did not join a church or pay his tithe. But because he believed and accepted who Jesus said he was, he was saved. From that day forward, he has been in Paradise with Jesus. I don't know where Paradise is. I think maybe it is a reception room where we wait until Jesus is ready to take us to Heaven. But it's okay because Jesus is there. How do I know? Because Jesus said so. I'm as sure as I am alive that my loved ones who died in the Lord—my parents, my daughter, and my husband—are there at this minute, with Jesus in Paradise, and have been since they drew their last breath. Honey, that's shoutin' words!

I hope you have seen Mary's boy. Mary's boy loves you and will not turn you away. Remember this, as Christians, we are told to walk in Jesus' footsteps. We are to conform to the very image of Christ. Today, we should be about the Father's business. I want to warn you—it may take you places you don't want to go. It may put you with people you really don't want to be with. The Pharisees certainly weren't about the Father's business.

The Father's business that Jesus was about was helping needy people. Feeding the hungry. Clothing the naked. Comforting the sick. Helping the homeless. Visiting the jails. Encouraging the downtrodden. When you do these things, 2000 years later, you are following in the footsteps of Jesus and you, too, are being about your Father's business.

CHAPTER 17

And God Created Woman

*Jane at her 85th birthday party on September 30, 2010
at the Clinton Library in Little Rock*

I TIMOTHY 3:11

And God Created Woman

A poem about the strength of women

CHARLES HASTINGS SMITH was a Nazarene Evangelist and a gifted poet. He wrote this poem and gave me permission to use it. I changed some verses and added others. Whenever I speak to a group, I get the names of 10-12 of their local women to fill in the blanks.

AND God Created Woman

Since then, women have made the difference
In life's great fantastic game.
They have come to walk gracefully among us
With fresh flowers in their hair.
And to touch our lives with beauty
And to scatter perfume everywhere.

So, today we call the roll of noble women
Who have changed the destinies of men.
And there are so many of these fair brave daughters...
Those living now, and those who lived back then.

Do you remember when Eve smiled at Adam,
And bore him two sons, Abel and his brother Cain?
And the birth of children became a wonder
And joy outweighed the pregnancy of pain.

Do you remember Rachel and her sister, Leah,
Women brave, beautiful, and bold.
And who can forget Hagar in the wilderness,
Or Sarah when she was old.

I can still hear the prayers of Esther
Crying, "Let me perish for the right."
I can see Ruth, the Moabitess,
Entreating Naomi in the night.

I can still hear the songs of Deborah,
Elizabeth, and Hannah, too.
I can see the good deeds of Abigail
Teaching us what obedience can do.

I can see Priscilla in Ephesus,
Full of faith and spirit-led.
And I hear a widow shouting in the land of Naine,
Because her son is no longer dead.

I have the greatest love for Claudia
And for Mary Magdalene...
She, from whom Christ drove seven devils,
Changed her life, and made her clean.

Jesus said it is hard for rich men
To enter into Heaven's door.
But the little widow dropped two coins in the plate
And made herself immortal for evermore.

I must tell you of Martha, and her sister Mary,
Who never owned a big hotel.
Just a simple cottage, but was so full of love
They entertained the son of God, Immanuel.

And God created woman,
And He was proud of what He saw.
And since then every man has been grateful...
Every husband, uncle, brother, nephew, and son-in-law...

I must tell of Helen Keller,
Born deaf, mute, and blind.
Let trumpets blow for Fanny Crosby,
Whose 8,000 hymns have blessed mankind.

I must tell you of Clara Barton,
And Evangeline Booth,
Who set her high button shoes in her father's
    Salvation Army footsteps,
And shook the tambourine of truth.

Then once again the Salvation Army chose a lady
As their general in 1986.
Because they knew there is nothing
That a woman can not fix.

Let us not forget Martha Washington,
Or Joan of Arc on a burning cross.
Three cheers for the first American flag
From the skillful fingers of Betsy Ross.

I try to forget Delilah
Gowned in silk and sensuous with spice.
Teaching us to shun temptation,
And never enter into a fool's paradise.

And God created woman,
And behold his work was good.
Since then women have walked like gowned angels
Down the avenues of brotherhood.

On that special night in winter
God hung a diadem
From the rafter of a barn
In a town called Bethlehem.

And there an unknown teen-aged Jewish virgin
Cried out in a cattle shed.
And suddenly the world was bathed in light
And with a love unlimited.

There amid the cattle and gentle oxen
In a manger hewn from wood.
God forever exalted woman,
And placed his sanctity on motherhood.

And God created woman.
What a gift to lonely man.
Wife, comrade, helpmate,
Keeping his house spic and span.

I can see Dorcas, full of good works.
And Lydia in Phillipi.
Miriam recommending Jocabed to Pharoah's daughter
When little Moses began to cry.

I see Rhoda in Jerusalem
Grandmother Lois and Eunice too.
Teaching young Timothy Christian virtues
And what a young man should say and do.

Sing the songs of Kate Smith, and Norma Zimmer.
And the music of Jenny Linn.
And of Joni Erickson, the paraplegic, conquering pain
Again, and again, yet again.

I must tell you of Anne Frank,
And of Florence Nightingale.
And courageous Molly Pitcher
Giving dying soldiers water from her pail.

I must tell you of Carrie Nation
And tell it again and again.
She, with her bonnet and her hatchet
Standing up to foul, drunken, wicked men.

I must tell you of Janie Diffee
And what her life has meant to me
And all the lessons I learned in childhood
As a granddaughter at her knee.

I cannot forget my crippled mother,
So fragile when she died...
But, now skips the green vales of Eden
Beyond the Isthmus, and across the tide.

Sing the songs of Sandi Patti,
And _____ with face so fair.*＊
(Name a woman in your group who sings. If none, then name Little Evie.)
And see how quickly you forget Bathsheba
And the atheist, Madilyn Murray O'Hare.

Sing the songs of Gloria Gaither
As she opens Heaven's gates.
And Julia Howe's "Battle Hymn of the Republic"
And "How Beautiful America" by Catherine Bates.

Read the poems of Emily Dickinson,
Elizabeth Barrett Browning, too.
Read the lines of Helen Steiner Rice
And let their message get through to you.

Read the books of Catherine Marshall
And Corrie Ten Boom.
They will add substance to your soul
And hang inspiration in your room.

Let's not forget the courageous
Susan B. Anthony
Who fought and won the right to vote
For you and me.

Would you like to dream and fantasize,
Yet do your mind no harm.
Then remember Snow White and Goldilocks,
And Rebecca of Sunnybrook Farm.

But somewhere write the names of _____ *
*(Four or five names of women in your group.)

Then, compare these, would you please...
With all the girls you see
On Saturday Night Live TV.

Let me tell you of Susanna Wesley whose sons, Charles and John
Were among the 19 children that she bore.
Teaching each one to love God supremely,
And become a spirit-filled troubadour.

Can you forget Ethel Waters
Or Mahalia Jackson, born poor and black
Who had a prayer closet in her bedroom
And made Heaven out of a three-room shack.

Go full circle with Mother Teresa,
She of the Catholic faith and oh!
The dedication she possessed
Made the poor of India love her so.

Let's remember Mrs. Billy Graham
A famous preacher's wife.
Who has kept the home fires burning
While her husband helped change lives.

There's Vonette Bright,
Who with her husband, Bill
Has proclaimed the Gospel message
Across the campus hill.

There's my daughters Janie and Vikki,
Who pointed their children toward God.
And all the other young mothers who lead their families
To walk where Jesus trod.

Rise up for Mrs. Johnson,
Who's Bible Study Fellowships through her prolific pen
Teaching God's Word around the world
To women and to men.

So, when you make your list of famous women,
What name do you put up there first?
Certainly not the name of Jezebel or Squeaky Fromm
Nor San Francisco's Patty Hearst.

Would your first choice be The Slinky Cher,

Or the oft-married Zsa Zsa Gabor.

Or some flirt on an afternoon soap opera,

Or the free swingin' punk rock gal who lives next door?

Would your first choice be Cleopatra,

The sultry goddess of the Nile?

Or the treacherous Josephine of France,

With cunning ways and carnal guile?

Would your first choice be Bonnie Parker,

Who rode and robbed with her boyfriend Clyde?

My first choice would be Mary, the mother of Jesus,

Who cried at the feet of the crucified.

Then I would add the name of Agnes Diffee,

My aunt who preached about God's grace.

Then, I'd write the name of _____

(The name of one woman in your group.)

God's love shines right from her face.

Give some praise to _____

(One to three names of women in your group.)

And give _____ a featured spot.

(One woman named in your group.)

And pin an orchid on _____. (One name.)

And give _____ a forget-me-not. (One name.)

Don't forget Roy Roger's wife, Dale Evans,

And all famous stars who witness to being born again.

And raise a flag for Anita Bryant,

Persecuted for her stand against sin.

Give a cheer for Willie Oates,
Whom I'll bet you that
She's given more time to charity than anyone!
Or I'll eat her hat.

Say a prayer for _____ (The first and last names of the President's wife)
And for _____ (The first and last names of the Governor's wife)
And every woman here
May God refresh you like the morning dew.

Let the world hear your witness,
Let it rise up with one accord.
Let your testimony ascend like a sweet incense
In the nostrils of the Lord.

Sing your song _____ handmaidens, (Name Group)
Sing it until nothing can suppress
The inward joy, that makes us all children,
Called into holiness.

Sing this song like holy women,
And when you leave this meeting room,
Sing it somewhere—where they least expect it.
Scatter sunshine in somebody's gloom.

Sing this song when you leave here.
Hang your jacket in the car.
But don't lock your song inside your handbag
Or some cosmetic jar.

Sing it as you drive down the highway.
Let it be your glad refrain.
Sing it when your family feels depression.
Then this meeting will not have been in vain.

Sing it some morning in the kitchen
When you feel discouraged and all alone.
Then sing it tomorrow when we gather
With God's great family around the throne.

Sing it there through golden eons,
Sing it with all those who possess.
The inheritance of the Christ-born,
The glorious experience of high holiness.

Sing it when you bow down before Him
To thank Him for his loving grace.
And, Christ will smile and say, "Well done, _____ Woman,
(Name Group)
You have made My world a better place."

There was never a day I did not believe in God and my faith lets me know—not think or believe—but *know* that I am a child of God, saved by the blood of Jesus Christ, with a home waiting for me in Heaven.

That's what makes old Jane tick!

G'nite!

CPSIA information can be obtained at www.ICGtesting.com
Printed in the USA
244747LV00002BA/2/P